PERSONAL VOCATION

PERSONAL VOCATION

VOCATION

GOD CALLS
EVERYONE BY NAME

Germain Grisez
Russell Shaw

Our Sunday Visitor Publishing Division
Our Sunday Visitor, Inc.
Huntington, Indiana 46750

Our Sunday Visitor Publishing Division
Our Sunday Visitor, Inc.
200 Noll Plaza
Huntington, IN 46750

ISBN: 1-59276-021-X (Inventory No. T72)
LCCN: 2003105060

Cover design by Monica Haneline
Cover images courtesy of RubberBall Productions
Interior design by Robert L. Hoffman

PRINTED IN THE UNITED STATES OF AMERICA

The authors gratefully dedicate this book to their parents, families, teachers, friends, and others who have helped them find and try to live out their personal vocations.

TABLE OF CONTENTS

INTRODUCTION

Every year in the spring the Church celebrates a World Day of Prayer for Vocations when Catholics are urged to storm heaven more than they are accustomed to do on behalf of this noble cause. In 2003 the fortieth of these annual observances fell on May 11, the Fourth Sunday of Easter. The theme was "Vocation to Service."

In his message for the 2003 vocations day, Pope John Paul II cited Jesus as the universal model of service. Then, having made this point, he joined it to vocation in these words:

> In the Bible, service is always linked to a specific call that comes from God. For this reason, it represents the greatest fulfillment of the dignity of the creature. . . . This was the case in the life of Jesus, too, the faithful Servant who was called to carry out the universal work of redemption.

Service, vocation, and the work of redemption: central in Jesus' life, central also in the lives of Jesus' followers. And not just vocation in a generic sense, but vocation in a sense that is special, unique, for each individual. The Holy Father continued:

> How can one not read in the story of the "servant Jesus" the story of every vocation: the story that the Creator has planned for every human being, the story that inevitably passes through the call to serve and culminates in the discovery of the new name, designed by God for each individual? In these "names," people can grasp

their own identity, directing themselves to that self-fulfillment which makes them free and happy.

These "names" are personal vocations.

That needs explaining of course. Personal vocation is enormously important yet probably not widely understood. We have written this book with the hope of remedying that.

Start with the basics. In creating us as human beings, God gives us the capacity to make free choices. Confronting two or more possibilities, we often say, "I could do this or do that," or "I could do this or not do it." Having thought it over, more or less, and sometimes struggled with our feelings, we make up our minds and carry out our choice, realizing that it is *ours* in a profound sense: we are responsible for it rather than just experiencing it.

Although God gives us this capacity to make free choices, He is not indifferent to the choices we make. We can make bad choices, do things that hurt others and ourselves, and even though God allows that, He does not want it. He always wants us to make good choices and has made that clear from the beginning. So when we choose and act wrongly, we disobey God. We sin.

Often, though, we need to choose between two or more good possibilities. Whichever we choose, we will not hurt others or ourselves, nor will we disobey God and sin. Is it *then* the case that God is indifferent to what we choose?

No, not at all.

Not all good possibilities are equally good. As a loving Father, God prefers that we choose the best. If we always did that, we would make the best use of our abilities, take advantage of the greatest opportunities, and benefit others and ourselves as richly as possible. And, as with our other good choices, we also would meet the most serious threats and challenges, and care for others and ourselves as effectively as we could.

God has given each of us a unique set of gifts. By revealing himself, especially in the life, death, and resurrection of Jesus, he also has given us far better possibilities than we would otherwise have had. Specifically, each of us is offered a unique role in the drama of salvation. By making the most of our gifts and playing our role well, we will make a contribution to the heavenly kingdom that no one else can make, and we will be all that we can be, not just in this life but forever.

This is what God wants. But, while commanding everyone to choose what is good rather than what is bad, he commands no one to choose what is better rather than what is good. Instead, he extends an invitation. He calls each of us by name, and if we listen to his call and try honestly to respond, he will guide each of us personally to what is best for us and everyone else.

Personal vocation is that divine calling and guidance. ⟩

1

ORGANIZING A LIFE

What does a personal vocation look like? Here's how a Catholic law-school professor described a favorite student:

> Phil had a body no one would covet. What the doctors called soft-bone disease had produced misshapen limbs, a slightly over-sized head, and legs that did not work. Since he couldn't walk, he got around in a motorized wheelchair.
>
> He was a native of a town in upstate New York who had entered our law school with the class of 1996. Health problems, including heart trouble, delayed his graduation a year.
>
> For reasons unknown to me, the disease exacted a great toll on his internal organs. But not on his brain. Phil's mind was fine — he was sharper than almost all his classmates. And he had an indomitable spirit. He was game.
>
> He volunteered to serve as an intern public defender representing misdemeanor defendants in county court. These aren't softhearted folks. With few exceptions, they are manipulators, predators. They typically complained that the court-paid public defenders weren't real lawyers. As for the students who helped the public defenders, they were far down on the food chain.
>
> Phil took the hardest assignment available, working in the basement of the jail in quarters so tight he couldn't move around in his

cart. He never hesitated, never faltered, never showed any self-consciousness about his looks or the way he got around.

As the faculty member in charge of the internship program, I was afraid the prisoners either wouldn't take him seriously or would make fun of him. Or both. I needn't have worried. None of the law student interns was as respected as Phil.

My admiration for him grew. A few weeks before graduation we had a long talk about his health and his plans. He was looking forward to practicing law. That was his dream, a dream he'd pursued doggedly. Now he was nine-tenths of the way there.

Even so, there was something odd about the way he spoke. At the time, I couldn't put my finger on it, and we never had another conversation like that. At the end of April, eating dinner with friends in the student center, Phil suddenly pitched out of his wheelchair. The paramedics said he was dead before he hit the floor.

A couple of weeks later there was a memorial service in the campus church. It was packed. There was a lot of speechmaking. But no one said, and I am pretty confident no one even thought, so much as a word about hopes disappointed, dreams unrealized, that kind of thing. Not a single word.

Several students reminisced about Phil's example of faith, courage, and good humor. Getting him up and running every day had been a group project. They'd helped out, and they obviously felt glad, even privileged, that they had. None of them spoke about loss. All spoke of gain — their own.

One of Phil's friends, an English instructor who'd lost his faith, said he felt himself being drawn back to the Church. What he'd found most mystifying about faith, he said, was the senselessness of evil and loss — why bad things happen to good people. But Phil's death had helped restore his faith in God, because it didn't imply waste or meaninglessness or a life that hadn't worked out.

I think we all understood that he was called to be a law student, a son, a brother, a friend, a football fan, a faithful son of the Church. But he was not called to be a lawyer.

Looking back on that talk he and I had, I think I know now what I only dimly sensed then. Phil understood that being a lawyer wasn't his main calling. I don't mean he had a premonition of his death. He was expecting to be a lawyer, at least for a while, and he would have been a fine one. But I now believe he had learned what we all need to learn: that we are called at this moment to do God's will — because it is his will. And at the next moment and the next. And so on, until the very last.

Phil was called to be a disabled person, someone with soft-bone disease. Sometime before I got to know him, he recognized and accepted that vocation. The next step for him would have been to be a lawyer with soft-bone disease, as he had been a law student — and also a son, friend, avid football fan, and loyal son of the Church, with soft-bone disease.

He wasn't preachy or pious. He just knew what God wanted him to be and decided to cooperate with that. Phil lived the heck out of his vocation, and when he died, it was mission accomplished.

Lord Chesterfield's Way

Phil's is one vocation story. But really to understand personal vocation, we need to spend time looking at some other, very different ways people have adopted for organizing their lives.

Lord Chesterfield, for one. This eighteenth-century British statesman and man of the world wrote a series of letters of advice to his illegitimate son — letters prized even today as literary gems. Indeed they are beautifully written. As for moral content, judge for yourself.

Writing in March, 1747, Lord Chesterfield encouraged his son to "lead a life of real, not of imaginary, pleasure." Explaining what that life was like, he said that if he had a chance to live the last thirty years over again he would pursue "the pleasures of the table, and of wine" but would take care to avoid the "pains" associated with excess in either. He would gamble for amusement and to rub elbows with fashionable people, but he would not gamble to the point of serious loss. He would spend some time reading and the rest of his time in the company of "people of sense and learning . . . chiefly those above me."

Such, remarked Lord Chesterfield, are "the pleasures of . . . people of fashion." He concluded with these memorable words: "A real man of fashion and pleasure observes decency; at least, neither borrows nor affects vices; and, if he unfortunately has any, he gratifies them with choice, delicacy, and secrecy." It is not recorded how Lord Chesterfield's illegitimate son responded to those words.

The Gospel According to Gail Sheehy

Much has changed since those days. But not everything.

Fast-forward to 1976. It was a year that brought many wondrous and not so wondrous events, among them the Bicentennial of the United States, the Jimmy Carter–Gerald Ford presidential campaign, and Legionnaire's Disease, a mysterious sickness that killed twenty-nine people attending a convention in Philadelphia. It also witnessed the publication of a book that was to become one of the most popular and influential of our times.

The volume was called *Passages* and was subtitled *Predictable Crises of Adult Life*. Its author was a journalist named Gail Sheehy.

A less than admiring observer of Sheehy's career, Franklin Foer of the liberal weekly *The New Republic,* recalls that Sheehy first came to national attention in the early 1970s with a five-part series in *New York* magazine about a Manhattan prostitute and her pimp. Soon, though, the author was forced to admit that the prostitute she wrote about didn't really exist but was a "composite." This was a fact she'd left out of her articles. The controversy that followed was a problem for Sheehy for a time, Foer writes, "but in 1976 she published a book of pop psychology called *Passages*, and its wild success — three years on *The New York Times'* best-seller list — gave her career a powerful boost." In her book, she propounded what Foer calls "Sheehy's totalizing theory of character." This is the notion that adulthood is organized around a series of "critical turning points along the life cycle when one's vulnerability is exaggerated but one's opportunity for growth is also heightened."

16

Passages has had several updatings and numerous spinoffs; after more than a quarter-century it remains in print. The reason for its enormous popularity is easy to see. Written in lively journalistic style, it preaches a gospel at once simple and compelling: Be fulfilled. And (within the bounds of legality no doubt) do whatever you have to do to accomplish that. *Passages* is the "you-only-go-round-once" philosophy in 393 very readable pages.

The book opens with a gripping introduction that explains its genesis. On assignment in Northern Ireland, Sheehy came close to being killed when British troops opened fire on Catholic civil rights marchers in Derry. This brush with death left Sheehy, only in her mid-thirties at the time, shaken, traumatized, haunted by horrible dreams. It took months for her nerves to settle. As they did, a new conviction dawned on her.

> As we reach midlife in the middle thirties or early forties, we become susceptible to the idea of our own perishability. If an accident that interrupts our life occurs at this time, our fears of mortality are heightened. We are not prepared for the idea that time can run out on us, or for the startling truth that if we don't hurry to pursue our own definition of a meaningful existence, life can become a repetition of trivial maintenance duties. . . . In my case, the unanticipated brush with death in Ireland brought the underlying issues of midlife forward in full force.

In this way the stage was set.

Looking to expand this new insight, ground it in something besides her own experience, and eventually produce a book, Sheehy turned to other sources. The crucial one was the work of Erik Erikson, a psychoanalyst who had been a friend and disciple of Sigmund Freud. (Erikson died in 1994 at the age of ninety-one.) In 1950 he published a study called *Childhood and Society* setting out in clear and accessible terms a "life-cycle" theory of human development organized around three stages of adulthood. Here is Sheehy's popularization of its key point:

> Erikson constructed a chart showing life unfolding in observable sequence. Each stage was marked by a crisis. "Crisis" connoted not a catastrophe, but a turning point, a crucial period of increased

vulnerability and heightened potential. . . . At such points either achievements are won or failures occur, leaving the future to some degree better or worse but in any case, restructured.

The other main sources for the writing of *Passages* were in-depth interviews conducted by Sheehy with scores of articulate, upscale Americans who had faced, and in most cases successfully navigated, midlife crises and moved on to a new stage in their quest for personal fulfillment. These personal histories are candid and consistently fascinating. Reading them is an exercise in journalistic voyeurism — commonplace now but not so common then — which the book's tone of therapeutic piety seemingly renders legitimate. Although the author tells the stories of both women and men, she is aggressively up front in her commitment to the feminist project of women's liberation.

Passages was the right book for a particular moment. It appeared at a time when many Americans had become acutely aware of themselves as better educated, more affluent, and more full of self-doubt than ever before. The first wave of post–World War II baby boomers, already schooled to nourish a sense of entitlement when it came to realizing their potential and doing as they pleased, were beginning to turn thirty and to ask themselves: So, what's next?

Passages Pro and Con

There are several things to say about all this.

One is that, at least in broad outline, Erik Erikson's life-cycle theory is hardly new; the seven-year itch is a familiar cliché. And, somewhat more elevated than that, the pages of history are filled with stories of people who at critical midpoints in their lives made momentous changes of direction of one kind or another. In the area of religion alone, one thinks of such diverse figures as Moses, Siddhartha Gautama (the Buddha), Mohammed, St. Augustine, Martin Luther, St. Ignatius Loyola, John Wesley, John Henry Newman, Edith Stein, and Charles Colson, the Watergate figure who became a committed Christian and devoted himself to prison ministry. Even Jesus experienced a momentous turning point on the occasion of his baptism by John around the age of thirty.

Beyond memorable personages like these, countless ordinary people have traversed passages of their own. Everyone has family members or friends who, well along in adult life, took dramatic steps in pursuit of self-fulfillment and change: going back to school, switching jobs or even careers, changing spouses, pulling up stakes and moving from one coast to the other, or in some other manner — or *several* manners, perhaps — launching radical new voyages of self-discovery after having reached a midpoint along the way. Some people seem to enact these rituals of change over and over throughout their lives.

As the long American love affair with the frontier suggests, precisely this willingness to experiment, to substitute the new for the old, whether that means taking up a new hobby or a new way of life — this openness to unexplored possibilities, blending at times with rootlessness and lack of tradition yet sometimes pointing to surprising discoveries in the search for self — has been part of the American character from the start. Erik Erikson gave it a basis in psychological theory, and Sheehy popularized and chronicled its operation in the lives of generally well-to-do Americans of the 1970s with smart, trendy names like Serena and Jeb, Marabel and Aaron, and with smart, trendy tastes to match. But the phenomenon existed long before Erikson and Sheehy called it to the attention of Serena, Jeb, Marabel, and Aaron, and told them how important it was that they cultivate it for themselves.

Without entirely buying into a psychological theory like this, one can agree that a well-rounded approach to personal development will make plenty of allowance for the desirability, indeed the necessity, of openness to change. Not only that. It will attempt to mesh the dynamics of psychological development with the dynamics of the spiritual life. Timidly standing pat, burying oneself in "trivial maintenance duties," and always seeking safety in the tried-and-true can be a prescription for sterility, premature aging, and psychic petrifaction.

At the same time, it is important to realize that advocacy of life-cycle dynamics assumes the existence of real options — genuine possibilities for significant change — and of persons psychologically, culturally, and (perhaps especially) economically equipped to capitalize on them. This approach is tailored to upscale baby-boomers and Generation X-ers in a society that prizes individualism and consumerism. The Serenas and Aarons of this world are people with the money and the social support systems to pursue self-realization as they choose. Poor people needn't apply.

Nor need people apply who have a well-developed sense of the obligations that flow from commitments made to others — commitments with respect to marriage and family life, a profession, a church. People for whom their own fulfillment is the fundamental principle in organizing their lives may act generously and altruistically. Or they may not. The really important thing, as Sheehy observes, is that they take those "fundamental steps of expansion that will open a person, over time, to the full flowering of his or her own individuality." *Full flowering of one's individuality* is the highest good.

It is also reasonable to ask whether a regimen of regular, radical change, appealing as it may be to some people, is healthy for all. That hardy spiritual classic *The Imitation of Christ* expresses an important truth when it remarks that "dreaming of a change of place has deceived many a person." True, the *Imitation* is speaking immediately and directly to fifteenth-century monks and nuns; but its insight into the perennial importance of the virtue of stability needs to be taken seriously by people in the twenty-first century as well: "Go here and there, where you will, you will never find perfect rest."

This pattern of ongoing, repeated change mirrors, on a very deep level of personality, the values of our postindustrial, information society. Managers today routinely require employees to learn new skills in order to compete in ever-shifting markets. Many companies and other institutions and organizations also employ sophisticated marketing strategies and advertising techniques intended to make consumers believe that they need and want (very often: need *because* they want) new versions of old goods and services, with the same end in view: ascendancy in the never-ending struggle for profit. No doubt this makes good sense in materialistic terms. That it always and in every case makes good sense in human terms is open to doubt.

Passages nevertheless makes some very valid points. People aren't meant to stew in misery and abandon all hope for change. But even so, the book ultimately is a sophisticated argument for selfishness. It gives scant encouragement to loyalty, to living a life of self-sacrificing service, to community and the common good. *Passages* is a guidebook for the Me Generation, with its single-minded focus on individual self-fulfillment. In a secularized society, this is what takes the place of the central principle animating people in societies where religious faith and values are strong: to love God above all things and to love one's neighbor as oneself. In the world of *Passages*, moreover, there is no room for personal vocations.

Although the book's Eriksonian orthodoxy is specific to itself, the approach it embodies is widespread these days — in school guidance programs for example, where the ideal held out to children and young people is essentially this: Clarify your values, set your priorities, line up your goals — and then go for it!

But let's be fair. This model is more or less consciously set in opposition to a desperate alternative that, paradoxically, can be seen at work in the lives of some poor, fundamentally hopeless, ghetto people and in those of some of the very rich. Lacking expectations for anything except what they already have, possessing no significant goals or lofty dreams, and finding themselves trapped in emptiness and despair, rich and poor alike may be driven to kill the pain with alcohol, drugs, sexual experimentation, and other vicious practices. Despite its deficiencies, the goal-directed paradigm of the school guidance-counselor at least attempts to offer young people a way to organize their lives that isn't directly self-destructive.

Coming of Age with Margaret Mead

Who best embodies the ideal of the life-cycle regimen of self-fulfillment promoted in *Passages?* Who has shown the way to the promised land? The answer comes at midpoint in Gail Sheehy's book in an adulatory profile of Margaret Mead, whom the author anoints in glowing terms as "the quintessential woman achiever."

Margaret Mead was born December 16, 1901, in Philadelphia, in a household of social scientists. After majoring in psychology at Barnard College, she received a doctorate in anthropology from Columbia University. Field work in American Samoa and in New Guinea led to best-selling books: *Coming of Age in Samoa* and *Growing Up in New Guinea.*

She was no armchair theorist. "For her," a biographical sketch on her 2001 Centennial website records, "anthropology was an urgent calling, a way to bring new understandings of human behavior to bear on the future." It was Mead's thesis that human development and the way human beings behave are largely determined by culture. The "civilized" world had much to learn from the "primitive," she insisted, especially where sex was concerned. She was, we are told, "the first anthropologist to look at human development in a cross-cultural perspective." It hardly needs saying that she was a cultural relativist to the core, proselytizing on behalf of the message that standards of right and wrong are malleable cultural artifacts, not unlike questions of cuisine and attire.

Mead, to repeat, was no mere theorist. She put her message to work in her private life. Gail Sheehy, lionizing the eminent anthropologist as "the General among the foot soldiers of modern feminism," notes among other things that before the age of forty-five she had "cooperated in three marriages" and in "an extraordinary joint household." Clearly, Mead knew without instruction what "passages" were all about. Sheehy writes:

> In her general's role she is a prophet in her own country. As a woman she was a deviant in her own culture. She had it all figured out more than fifty years ago. . . . Mead has very little patience with people whose capacities are impaired by wrestling with their private hells. She has conquered her own or ignored them. Why can't the minions march briskly out of their barbarous suburbs over the bones of their charred marriages, gather up their freaked-out children, admit the nuclear family was an experiment in disaster, and get on with the job done right? What is holding them back?

Not a lot seems to have held back Margaret Mead. Her first marriage was to a minister. It suited her for a while because it gave her "what she wanted: a marriage with no obstacles to being herself" (the minister commented that he needed an appointment to see her). Her second marriage was to an anthropologist from New Zealand. Sheehy writes: "Her choice, as always, was educated by Margaret Mead's vision of Margaret Mead." Her third marriage was to British anthropologist Gregory Bateson.

At thirty-eight ("sheltered by age and reputation from the havoc such an event can play with a career") Mead had a child. She proved to be a conscientious and devoted mother — in her own inimitable fashion. On one occasion, she proudly wrote, she and Bateson actually "took care of [the baby] for a whole weekend." Otherwise nannies did the job.

Eventually Mead and Bateson merged households with another married couple. Mead left all childcare and household work to the other woman. "I just thought it was easier to leave her in charge. I was terribly busy," she explained. In 1945, she divorced Bateson, "tore up much of the personal and professional structure that had sustained the first half of her life and began building a new support system." A large part of it turned out to be a quarter-century-long lesbian relationship with anthropologist Ruth Benedict.

The *Journal of Lesbian Studies* hails Mead and Benedict as "two of the most influential women in 20th-century social science." An admiring notice of a book-length study of their liaison says they "used their anthropological studies to call attention to the cultural foundations of American life, Benedict seeking to make the world more tolerant of deviance and Mead to liberate the individual from the artificial constraints of gender and race." Along with people like Planned Parenthood founder Margaret Sanger and sex researcher Alfred Kinsey, Margaret Mead was a pioneer in the sexual revolution that turned roles, relationships, and patterns of behavior between the sexes upside down and inside out in the middle years of the twentieth century. A liberal icon with the status of a cult figure in her own day, she remains a historical presence of considerable importance even now.

Mead wrote twenty books and co-authored as many more. Not everyone is impressed with her work. The Intercollegiate Studies Institute calls *Coming of Age in Samoa* the worst nonfiction volume of the century for its sloppy scholarship. Defenders of traditional values who understand the positions she held and the role she played in twentieth-century America regard her as a destructive figure — a person who did more than her share to bring about the present moral chaos.

Nevertheless, Margaret Mead reached a huge audience of middle-class women through a column in *Redbook* magazine. She was an inveterate lecturer, conference-goer, and giver of interviews. She received twenty-eight honorary degrees, and after her death in 1978 was awarded the Presidential Medal of Freedom. The reality of the freedom she exemplified may not have been too well understood by the bestowers of this award, but surely Mead's individuality flowered throughout her long life. "The delights of self-discovery are always available," Gail Sheehy helpfully informs her readers. Where these particular delights are concerned, Margaret Mead was a prophetic figure.

The Taliban Fighter Down the Block

But not the only one. Echoes of preoccupation with self-discovery and individualistic self-fulfillment can be heard in the sad story of John Walker Lindh, "the American Taliban," and his family.

Lindh is the young American who converted to Islam, went to Yemen and Pakistan to study the Koran, and wound up soldiering with the Taliban. In December 2001, he was dragged, filthy and wounded, from a medieval fortress in northern Afghanistan along with other fighters. He was twenty years old at the time. Ten months later he was sentenced to twenty years in prison.

When John Walker Lindh's story first came to light, Americans shook their heads in wonderment that an American boy could have gotten himself into such a fix. But even though Lindh's trajectory was unquestionably bizarre, it may not have been all that mystifying.

His parents, Frank and Marilyn, grew up in the counterculture of the 1960s, but by the time John was born in February, 1981, they had settled into middle-class life in the Washington, D.C., suburb of Takoma Park, Maryland — a community which *The Washington Post* calls "that small, nuclear-free municipality that so often marches to the beat of a different activist." In a nostalgic gesture toward the good old days, the Lindhs named the second of their three children John, partly in honor of Beatle John Lennon, who had been shot to death by a mentally disturbed fan two months before the baby's birth.

The Lindhs attended a Catholic church near their home and took up mildly liberal causes. A former neighbor described them to the *Post* as "very earnest, very nice, very intellectual." Another said: "They were liberal in the classic sense. They said they really wanted to let their children develop by giving them different experiences."

Young John attended a neighborhood elementary school, and then transferred to a "gifted and talented" program some distance away. A major family upheaval occurred when he was ten and Frank Lindh, having gotten a law degree, took a job in San Francisco. The Lindhs headed west, settling into a newly purchased home in San Anselmo, California, in wealthy, suburban Marin County. "The joke about Marin," says the *Post,* "is that it is a California cliché, a hot-tub haven that values nothing as much as self-discovery."

According to *Time* magazine, "the transition to California went badly" for young John. The boy bounced around from school to school, and spent two years "virtually a shut-in" because of poor health. After five months in the local high school, he switched to an experimental school where students met one-on-one with teachers once or twice a week instead of going to class. Somewhere along the way he acquired an interest in Islam. He began spending hours in Internet chat rooms trading questions and comments with others who shared this new enthusiasm.

There were other changes. His father went to work for Pacific Gas and Electric Company. His mother gave up Catholicism and became a Buddhist (she also had an interest in Native American rites). In 1997, aged sixteen, John dropped out of his progressive high school, passed a state proficiency examination to get a diploma, and announced that his name was Suleyman and he was a Muslim. San Anselmo residents, says *Time,* "did not get especially worked up" at seeing "tall, awkward, teenage John strolling the streets in Islamic dress." A family friend described his parents as "very supportive." A next door neighbor said of them all: "They were very kind people, very intelligent. They were all doing their own thing."

Not long after, John announced that he was going to Yemen to study Arabic so that he could read the Koran in the original and immerse himself in Islamic culture. The Lindhs worried but let him go. In a letter to his mother, written from Yemen in September, 1998, John suggested that the bombings of U.S. embassies in Africa the previous month "seem far more likely to have been carried out by the American government than by any Muslims."

Returning home on a visit in early 1999, he found that much had changed. His parents' marriage, troubled for years, was in a state of collapse. Late in 1998 Frank Lindh had declared that he was gay and moved out. In June of 1999, shortly after John's return, Frank filed for divorce, and a few days later the Lindhs sold the house in San Anselmo. Within a few months John was back in Yemen studying at an Islamic university. After terrorists bombed the USS Cole during a refueling visit to Yemen in October 2000, killing seventeen sailors and injuring more than twice as many more, Frank Lindh got a message from his son saying the American vessel had no business being in an Islamic country.

Next John turned up in Islamabad, capital of Pakistan. Around the middle of 2001 he headed for Afghanistan, where he signed up as a Taliban soldier. According to his attorneys, he never fired a weapon but only served as a guard. After U.S. bombing began in November in response to the 9/11 attacks on the World Trade Center and the Pentagon, John/Suleyman joined his Taliban comrades in retreat. Speaking to a CNN interviewer from a hospital bed after his capture, he said about what had happened, "It's exactly what I thought it would be."

In July, 2002, under a plea-bargain agreement, John Walker Lindh pleaded guilty in U.S. district court in Alexandria, Virginia, to one count of providing services to the Taliban and one count of carrying explosives during a felony. On October 4 the district judge sentenced him to twenty years. The young man said he hadn't gone to Afghanistan to fight against America and didn't support terrorism; but, he conceded, "I made a mistake by joining the Taliban."

Certainly John Walker Lindh is an extreme case. Yet in its own way the path he traced for himself in little more than two decades sums up confusions that bedevil many people today — uncertainties about meaning and fulfillment, and how to organize a life. Here is the dark side of the delights of self-discovery. Bear in mind that the Lindhs were "kind people, very intelligent . . . all doing their own thing."

A Better Way

We need a better way of organizing our lives.

The way described in this book is personal vocation. But immediately we confront a problem. Many people, perhaps Catholics most of all, equate vocation with a calling to the priesthood or consecrated life.

(A note about terminology. By "the priesthood" here and wherever the context does not indicate otherwise, we mean the ordained — or ministerial — priesthood, rather than the priesthood in which all the baptized share. That common priesthood, though not itself a vocation, is at the source of every personal vocation. By "consecrated life" here and throughout the book, we mean not only what is usually called "religious life" but also the other forms of life recognized by the Church that are undertaken by a commitment to practice chastity, poverty, and obedience for the kingdom's sake.)

Although the priesthood and the various forms of consecrated life are indeed vocations, in a sense to be explained below, they aren't the only ones. To assume otherwise not only misses the full reality of vocation but discourages people who are not called to the vocations of priesthood or consecrated life from seeking to discern, accept, and live out *their* vocations and responsibilities as members of the lay faithful, who are the overwhelming majority of the People of God.

For example, early in 2002, a prominent national vocations official issued a statement calling on the "people in the pews" in parishes across the United States and Canada to pray and work for vocations. These people in the pews, he explained, are "people who work beside the future vocations in our Church. These are the people who pray next to them. These are the people who know who they are. . . . These future vocations of the Church just need to be invited." In other words, the people in the pews should invite the people who have vocations to the priesthood and consecrated life to heed the call.

No doubt the priest who said that is a serious-minded man engaged in important work — encouraging men and women to become priests and religious. But with all due respect to him and the cause he represents, his way of putting the matter — opposing certain Catholics who supposedly are *without* vocations to certain other Catholics who *have* them — fundamentally misstates reality in a way that does great harm.

27

Start with the central fact that many people in the pews — at least, all who want to carry out God's will for them and who sometimes wonder what that is — are responding to vocations of their own. It isn't just individuals with callings to priesthood and consecrated life ("the future vocations of our Church") who have vocations. *Every member of the Church who seeks to know what God asks of him or her will discover a unique personal vocation of his or her own.*

There obviously is a vocations crisis in the Church today. But, contrary to what often is said, there is no vocations shortage. A shortage of vocations in the Church is literally impossible. The issue is not whether a select few will receive vocations at some point in the future, but whether all members of the Church will recognize, embrace, and live out the vocations they have. If members of the Church in general do that — but *only* if they do it — the misnamed shortage of vocations will be over.

Is this an eccentric and possibly dangerous way of thinking about vocations? No, for as it happens, it is the way Pope John Paul II thinks.

Here is what he said in his message for the 2001 World Day of Prayer for Vocations: "Every life is a vocation, and every believer is invited to cooperate in building up the Church." And here he is in the 1989 document in which he drew together insights and conclusions from the 1987 session of the Synod of Bishops:

> The fundamental objective of the formation of the lay faithful is an ever-clearer discovery of one's vocation and the ever-greater willingness to live it so as to fulfill one's mission.
>
> *God calls me and sends me forth* as a laborer in his vineyard. He calls me and sends me forth to work for the coming of his Kingdom in history. This personal vocation and mission defines the dignity and the responsibility of each member of the lay faithful and makes up the focal point of the whole work of formation, whose purpose is the joyous and grateful recognition of this dignity and the faithful and generous living-out of this responsibility.
>
> In fact, from eternity God has thought of us and has loved us as unique individuals. Every one of us he called by name, as the

28

Good Shepherd "calls his sheep by name" (Jn 10:3). However, only in the unfolding of the history of our lives and its events is the eternal plan of God revealed to each of us. Therefore, it is a gradual process; in a certain sense, one that happens day by day. (On the Vocation and the Mission of the Lay Faithful in the Church and in the World, *Christifideles Laici,* n. 58)

That entire document is specifically about the Catholic laity. And it is clear from this passage and many other statements by John Paul that he understands personal vocation to be a central reality in the life of every member of the Church without exception, including those who are lay people: "Every one of us he called by name."

"I Wanted Life . . . for Others, Too"

There are many different callings, but all are called.

Phil the law student is one instance. Dorothy Day, co-founder of the Catholic Worker movement, is another.

Looking back from the vantage point of years, Dorothy Day recalled her growing sense of identification with the poor and destitute at the age of fifteen as she read books like *The Jungle,* Upton Sinclair's expose of the meatpacking industry, and studied the lives and careers of early Russian proponents of radical social change. The romantic figure of Prince Peter Kropotkin especially captured her fancy.

This Russian nobleman, who died in 1921, became an anarchist, renounced his title, and devoted himself to serving the peasants. Kropotkin, Day wrote, "brought to my mind the plight of the poor, of the workers." And even though her own experience of the destitute was, up to then, limited to reading about them, nevertheless "the very fact that *The Jungle* was about Chicago where I lived, whose streets I walked, made me feel that from then on my life was to be linked to theirs, their interests were to be mine; I had received a call, a vocation, a direction to my life." Indeed she had. But she would be a long time working it out.

Dorothy Day was born November 8, 1897, in Brooklyn, the third of four children. While she was still a child, her newspaperman father moved the family to Berkeley, California, and later to Oakland, not so far from the Marin County community where, decades later, John Walker Lindh attended a high school without classes and converted to Islam.

Day recalls those days in her autobiography, *The Long Loneliness.* "We did not search for God when we were children. We took him for granted," she writes. The family was believing but not particularly religious, and "I do not remember going to church in those years." All the same, the young girl had a deep, intuitive religious sense.

She recalls one rainy Sunday afternoon spent reading the Bible, when she was struck with a profound sense of "handling something holy."

A Methodist friend took her to Sunday school and church. "I believed, but I did not know in what I believed." But the San Francisco earthquake and fire of 1906 created in the child a distorted idea of God — "a tremendous Force, a frightening impersonal God, a Voice, a Hand stretched out to seize me, His child, and not in love."

Her father's job kept the family on the move. Soon the Days were in Chicago, where young Dorothy became friends with a Catholic girl. As they sat on the back porch together one night, her friend told her the life of a saint. Later, she could not remember the name of the saint or even any of the saint's life, but she did recall her "feeling of lofty enthusiasm, and how my heart almost burst with desire to take part in such a high endeavor." Another time she found a Catholic neighbor on her knees praying. Dorothy began doing the same thing at home, and insisted her younger sister join her. "So we began to practice being saints — it was a game with us."

While she was in high school, one of her brothers went to work for a leftwing newspaper. Reading it, the girl learned about the labor leaders and radical agitators of the day, about the Industrial Workers of the World and Eugene Debs, about the struggles of the workers and the poor. She sensed that her future was tied up with them. But she also began to think of religion as more hindrance than help, since the churchgoing people she knew appeared complacent, comfortable, and lacking in concern for those in need.

Children look at things very directly and simply. I did not see anyone taking off his coat and giving it to the poor. I didn't see anyone having a banquet and calling in the lame, the halt and the blind. And those who were doing it, like the Salvation Army, did not appeal to me. I wanted, though I did not know it then, a synthesis. I wanted life and I wanted the abundant life. I wanted it for others too.

Joining the Socialist party was a natural step for her a year later when she went to the University of Illinois. Working for her board, she took her meals with the family of a Methodist professor and often discussed religion with these kindly souls. "But even as I talked about religion I rejected religion." Religious people lacked her burning commitment to the poor. "I felt at the time that religion would only impede my work."

Leaving school, she spent a year as a nurse at King's County Hospital in Brooklyn. The work was rewarding, but it was not for her. "A longing to write, to be pursuing the career of a journalist which I had chosen for myself, swept over me. . . . I loved the work in the hospital [but] I felt that it was a second choice, not my vocation. My work was to write."

And write she did, bouncing from Marxist newspapers to the *New Orleans Item*. She published a novel, sold the movie rights for $5,000, and went back to New York. Buying a small beach house on Staten Island, she settled into a common-law marriage with a British anarchist named Forster and made friends with writers and intellectuals like Alan Tate, Caroline Gordon, and the poet Hart Crane.

Her desire to serve the poor was intense and growing. And strange to say, as time went by it more and more seemed to point her in the direction of the Catholic Church. For it had begun to look to her like the real-life Church of the poor.

My very experience as a radical, my whole make-up, led me to want to associate myself with others, with the masses, in loving and praising God. Without even looking into the claims of the Catholic Church, I was willing to admit that for me she was the one true Church. . . . Far from being dead, she claimed and held the allegiance of the masses of people in all the cities where I had lived. They poured in and out of her doors.

But the attachment to Forster held her back. Although they had a daughter, Tamar, by now, Forster would not hear of marrying in the Church. In her second biography *From Union Square to Rome,* she writes "Becoming a Catholic would mean facing life alone, and I clung to family life. It was hard to contemplate giving up a mate in order that my child and I could become members of the Church. [Forster] would have nothing to do with religion or with me if I embraced it. So I waited."

But she knew it couldn't last. "If I could have felt that communism was the answer to my desire for a cause, a motive, a way to walk in, I would have remained as I was. But I felt that only faith in Christ could give the answer." She met a simple, elderly nun, Sister Aloysia, who gave her the *Messenger of the Sacred Heart* and the catechism to read — as supplements to Augustine, Pascal, and Dostoyevsky. One summer day she had Tamar baptized. A year later, in 1927, she entered the Church herself. Forster was gone for good.

A Catholic now, Dorothy found discontentment returning. "One must live in a state of permanent dissatisfaction with the Church," she concluded. The particular targets of her critique were "businesslike priests," "collective wealth," "the lack of a sense of responsibility for the poor" and the acceptance on the part of institutional Catholicism of the oppression of the poor by "our industrialist-capitalist order."

> I felt that charity was a word to choke over. Who wanted charity? And it was not just human pride but a strong sense of man's dignity and worth, and what was due him in justice, that made me resent, rather than feel proud of so mighty a sum total of Catholic institutions. . . . How I longed to make a synthesis reconciling body and soul, this world and the next, the teachings of Prince Peter Kropotkin and Prince Demetrius Gallitzin, who had become a missionary priest in rural Pennsylvania.

She had no regrets about becoming a Catholic, but she had no idea where she fit in.

By 1932 the country was deep in the Great Depression. In December Dorothy went to Washington as a journalist to cover a hunger march organized partly by the communists. Watching the marchers, she felt proud of them and ashamed of the lack of leadership by her Church and of her own failure to be involved. "How little, how puny my work had been since becoming a Catholic, I thought." As she writes in *From Union Square to Rome,* when the demonstration was over and she had filed her story, she realized that the feast of the Immaculate Conception was the next day, and went to the National Shrine of the Immaculate Conception to assist at Mass. "And the prayer that I offered up was that some way would be shown me, some way would be opened up for me to work for the poor and the oppressed," she says. As she knelt praying, it struck her that up to that point in her life as a Catholic she did not personally know even one Catholic lay person.

She returned to New York. "When I walked into my apartment, I found waiting for me a short, stocky man in his mid-fifties, as ragged and rugged as any of the marchers I had left." The man was a French peasant, an ardent Catholic, who spoke vividly about building a new culture — a new world — founded on justice and love and the message and model of Jesus Christ. He called his blend of Catholicism and radical social thought the "green revolution." His name was Peter Maurin, and he wanted Dorothy to join him.

Neither of them knew it then, but the Catholic Worker movement had just been born.

Peter Maurin died in 1949. Dorothy Day lived on until 1980. Sometimes she was a controversial figure — for example, because of the Catholic Worker movement's unyielding pacifism during World War II. Increasingly, though, she became a revered presence who exerted a profound influence on two generations of American Catholics by her word and example. The story of her Catholic Worker years is told in another book, *Loaves and Fishes.* But the movement's roots in her long struggle to find, accept, and begin to live out her personal vocation are clear in *The Long Loneliness.*

Near the end of it she shares with the reader something she had come to see while on a retreat:

Faith that works through love is the mark of the supernatural life. God always gives us a chance to show our preference for Him. With Abraham it was to sacrifice his only son. With me it was to give up my married life with Forster. You do these things blindly, not because it is your natural inclination — you are going against nature when you do them — but because you wish to live in conformity with the will of God.

For Dorothy Day, as for everyone else, the struggle to find and conform to the will of God in every single aspect of life is the indispensable essence of personal vocation.

The Idea of Personal Vocation

The answer to the vocation crisis of the Church is personal vocation. Rather than there being a shortage of vocations, as is often mistakenly supposed, there is a widespread failure by Catholics to seek, discern, accept, and live out their personal vocations. To a considerable extent it comes from failure to realize that there *is* such a thing as personal vocation.

Many Catholics hold a view of vocations from out of the past. It assumes that a vocation is a calling to the priesthood or consecrated life, and that people called to be priests and religious have vocations while people not called to those vocations have no vocation at all. It is imperative that Catholics get rid of that way of thinking once and for all and replace it with the awareness that everybody in the Church has a vocation. Only when that happens will the crisis of vocations — including the shortfall of those responding to their vocations to priesthood and consecrated life — be on its way to being solved.

Not only does everyone in the Church have a vocation, but everyone lives in a complex, rich vocational context. *Vocation* has at least three distinct senses, each relevant to every Catholic without exception. We can think of these three meanings as something like concentric circles, with each of the two outer rings further specifying what comes before it.

34

1. First is the vocation to be a Christian and to live the truth of one's faith. Thus, this is the calling to love God, love neighbor, do one's part to bring about the kingdom of God, and participate in the mission of the Church, which is Jesus' primary means for continuing his redemptive activity throughout history. But now with our help: "Go therefore and make disciples of all nations, baptizing them in the name of the Father and of the Son and of the Holy Spirit, teaching them to observe all that I have commanded you; and lo, I am with you always, to the close of the age" (Mt 28:19).

2. Next is vocation in the sense of state of life: the priesthood, consecrated life organized by the practice of the evangelical counsels (chastity, poverty, obedience), the married state, and so on. In everyday speech, state of life also commonly refers to things like a person's work and whether he or she is married or single. But, one author notes, "for a Christian, the term should have a much richer meaning, for it implies a position in life that a person holds not by accident or even by simple personal preference, but essentially by a divine choice, within a plan of love drawn up by God." When people speak of vocation, they often mean state of life and are referring to priesthood and consecrated life, as if these were the only vocations — or at least the only ones that count.

3. Finally, vocation in the sense of personal vocation. This is the unique, unrepeatable role God calls each baptized person to play in carrying out the all-embracing divine plan. As state of life is a specification of the fundamental Christian vocation, so personal vocation is a further specification of both of the above — the fundamental calling to love God and neighbor that comes with baptism and the special network of commitments, relationships, and responsibilities characteristic of a particular state of life. Personal vocation extends to the whole of life: it takes in all one's circumstances — strengths and weaknesses, talents and disabilities, existing commitments and obligations — and requires that all one's choices be made in their light.

Personal vocation is what Pope John Paul II refers to, for example, in his 1979 encyclical *Redemptor Hominis* (The Redeemer of Man), when he speaks of "the individual Christian's vocation" and the "singular, unique and unrepeatable grace by which each Christian in the community of the People of God builds up the Body of Christ" (n. 21).

The Pope attributes this insight in a special way to the Second Vatican Council (1962–65) and its fresh emphasis on the rights and duties within the People of God of all members of the Church. At its heart, this is an insight that concerns the crucial importance of personal vocation in the lives of individuals and in the life of the Church.

> This fidelity to the vocation received from God through Christ involves the joint responsibility for the Church for which the Second Vatican Council wishes to educate all Christians. Indeed, in the Church as the community of the People of God under the guidance of the Holy Spirit's working, each member has "his own special gift," as Saint Paul teaches (1 Cor 7:7). Although this "gift" is a personal vocation and a form of participation in the Church's saving work, it also serves others, builds the Church and the fraternal communities in the various spheres of human life on earth. (*Redemptor Hominis*, n. 21)

The enormous importance of personal vocation, for individuals and for the community of faith, is far from universally understood and appreciated. With this book, we hope to encourage a better, wider understanding. The subject could hardly be more important; for as Pope John Paul told the clergy of Rome at the start of Lent 2002, "every human life is the fruit of God's call and can only be positively fulfilled as a response to this call."

Ultimately, God's call and our response come together in our personal vocations.

2

A Historical Overview
of Personal Vocation

It is hardly something new for people to have personal vocations. But what about the *idea* of personal vocation — is this something very new or very old? The answer seems to be: a bit of both.

The idea is new in the sense that only in modern times — and quite recently in the Catholic Church — has it taken shape within a well-developed theology of vocation and an updated, well-rounded vision of the Church, the role of the laity, and related matters. But it is old in the sense that its kernel can be found in classic sources that go back very far.

It would be misleading, however, to suggest that the idea of personal vocation has a prominent role in the Old Testament. The dominant idea there is that God calls a *people* and makes a covenant with them collectively. In this era, no particular individual has a monopoly on the people's role, which is to be faithful to the covenant and to obey God's law. Upon hearing the law announced by Moses, the people reply, "All that the Lord has spoken we will do, and we will be obedient" (Ex 24:7). For the people in general, that seems to be enough.

Throughout the Old Testament, nevertheless, God summoned certain men and women to special roles, among them prophet, priest, and leader. "Moses alone shall come near to the Lord," God says (Ex 24:2). Moses' special role is to receive the law and announce it to the people.

He was not the only person specially summoned. Prophets, too, were individually called. Jeremiah, for example:

> Now the word of the Lord came to me saying, "Before I formed you in the womb I knew you, and before you were born I consecrated you; I appointed you a prophet to the nations." Then I said, "Ah, Lord God! Behold, I do not know how to speak, for I am only a youth." But the Lord said to me, "Do not say, 'I am only a youth'; for to all to whom I send you you shall go, and whatever I command you you shall speak. Be not afraid of them, for I am with you to deliver you," says the Lord. (Jer 1:4–8)

And Isaiah relates:

> Then flew one of the seraphim to me, having in his hand a burning coal which he had taken with tongs from the altar. And he touched my mouth, and said: "Behold, this has touched your lips; your guilt is taken away, and your sin forgiven." And I heard the voice of the Lord saying, "Whom shall I send, and who will go for us?" Then I said, "Here am I! Send me." And he said, "Go, and say to this people. . . ." (Is 6:6–9)

Rulers, too, were individually called. For example, David, whom the Lord selects after his seven seemingly more promising brothers are considered and rejected.

> And Jesse made seven of his sons pass before Samuel. And Samuel said to Jesse, "The Lord has not chosen these. . . . Are all your sons here?" And he said, "There remains yet the youngest, but behold, he is keeping the sheep." And Samuel said to Jesse, "Send and fetch him" . . . And the Lord said, "Arise, anoint him; for this is he." Then Samuel took the horn of oil, and anointed him in the midst of his brothers; and the Spirit of the Lord came mightily upon David from that day forward. (1 Sam 16:10–13)

The calling of Samuel himself — priest, prophet, and judge — is a striking story of personal vocation.

> At that time Eli, whose eyesight had begun to grow dim . . . was lying down in his own place; the lamp of God had not yet gone out, and Samuel was lying down within the temple of the Lord, where the ark of God was. Then the Lord called, "Samuel! Samuel!" and he said, "Here I am!" and ran to Eli, and said, "Here I am, for you called me." But he said, "I did not call; lie down again." (1 Sam 3:2–5)

The same thing happens another two times. The third time, Eli realizes it is the Lord who is calling the youth.

> Therefore Eli said to Samuel, "Go, lie down; and if he calls you, you shall say, 'Speak, Lord, for thy servant hears.'" So Samuel went and lay down in his place. And the Lord came and stood forth, calling as at other times, "Samuel! Samuel!" And Samuel said, "Speak, for thy servant hears." (1 Sam 3:9–10)

In due course it became clear to "all Israel from Dan to Beersheba . . . that Samuel was established as a prophet of the Lord" (1 Sam 3:20).

John Henry Newman, in a sermon preached in the 1830s, underlined the place of personal vocation in Samuel's story:

> Samuel was . . . marked from his birth as altogether an instrument of the Lord's providing. A similar providence is observable in the case of other favoured objects and ministers of God's mercy, in order to show that that mercy is entirely of grace. . . . God called him, in the sacred time, between night and morning, "Samuel, Samuel," and pronounced through him a judgment against Eli, for his sinful indulgence towards his sons. . . . Had Samuel grown to manhood before he was inspired, it would not have clearly appeared how far the work was immediately Divine; but when an

untaught child was made to prophesy against Eli, the aged high priest, the people were reminded, as in the case of Moses, who was slow of speech, that it was the Lord who "made man's mouth, the dumb, or deaf, the seeing, or the blind"; and that age and youth were the same with Him when his purposes required an instrument.

People do not give themselves personal vocations; these callings come from God, and they bring serious obligations with them.

Just how serious the obligations of a personal vocation can be is suggested in the New Testament by Jesus' parable of the talents (see Mt 25:14–30). "You wicked and slothful servant!" the master exclaims to the man who doesn't make a profit on the talent entrusted to him. And the master orders: "Cast the worthless servant into the outer darkness; there men will weep and gnash their teeth" (Mt 25:26, 30).

Personal Vocation in the New Testament

The situation in the New Testament is the same as the situation in the Old in some ways, but significantly different in others. Some selected individuals plainly are called to extraordinary roles in God's redemptive plan — for example, Mary, Joseph, the Twelve — and the Gospels make a point of carefully depicting Jesus' individual callings of several apostles. One of the liveliest accounts, placed at the start of John's Gospel (see Jn 1:35–50), was singled out for comment by the bishops of the United States in their 1992 collective pastoral letter *Stewardship: A Disciple's Response,* which contains what may be the American bishops' most specific endorsement yet of the idea of personal vocation.

Christians are called to be good stewards of the personal vocations they receive. Each of us must discern, accept, and live out joyfully and generously the commitments, responsibilities, and roles to which God calls him or her. The account of the calling of the first disciples, near the beginning of John's gospel, sheds light on these matters.

40

John the Baptist is standing with two of his disciples — Andrew and, according to tradition, the future evangelist John — when Jesus passes by. "Behold," John the Baptist exclaims, "the Lamb of God!" Wondering at these words, his companions follow Christ.

"What are you looking for?" Jesus asks them. "Rabbi," they say, "where are you staying?" "Come and you will see." They spend the day with him, enthralled by his words and by the power of his personality.

Deeply moved by this experience, Andrew seeks out his brother Simon and brings him to Jesus. The Lord greets him: "You will be called Kephas" — Rock. The next day, encountering Philip, Jesus tells him: "Follow me." Philip finds his friend Nathanael and, challenging his skepticism, introduces him to the Lord. Soon Nathanael too is convinced: "Rabbi, you are the Son of God; you are the King of Israel." . . .

[This narrative illuminates] the personal nature of a call from Jesus Christ. He does not summon disciples as a faceless crowd but as unique individuals. "How do you know me?" Nathanael asks. "Before Philip called you," Jesus answers, "I saw you under the fig tree." He knows people's personal histories, their strengths and weaknesses, their destinies; he has a purpose in mind for each one.

This purpose is individual vocation. "Only in the unfolding of the history of our lives and its events," says Pope John Paul II, "is the eternal plan of God revealed to each of us" (*Christifideles Laici*, n. 58). Every human life, every personal vocation, is unique.

One of the most famous accounts of a personal calling is the conversion of St. Paul. So deep was the impression it made on the early Christian community that it appears three times in the Acts of the Apostles. The first version goes like this:

Now as he journeyed he approached Damascus, and suddenly a light from heaven flashed about him. And he fell to the ground and heard a voice saying to him, "Saul, Saul, why do you persecute me?" And he said, "Who are you, Lord?" And he said, "I am Jesus, whom you are persecuting; but rise and enter the city, and you will be told what you are to do." (Acts 9:3–6)

Temporarily blinded, Saul (later to be Paul) goes to Damascus where he is received by a Christian named Ananias and recovers his sight. "And in the synagogues immediately he proclaimed Jesus, saying, 'He is the Son of God' " (Acts 9:20). Thus began the work of announcing the Good News to which he was to dedicate the rest of his life.

It is not just Jesus' followers who have vocations. From the New Testament it is clear that Jesus himself had a personal vocation, and the story told in the Gospels is the story of his living it out, in perfect fidelity to his Father's will. If we were to sum up Jesus' vocation in a word, it would be "Savior." As he says in John 12:46–47, "I have come as light into the world, that whoever believes in me may not remain in darkness. . . . I did not come to judge the world but to save the world." Jesus' personal vocation lay in overcoming death and sin, and communicating God's life to fallen human beings by establishing a new covenant between them and God. This was the mission he received from his Father and carried out all through his life, from childhood to resurrection and ascension into heaven.

As man, Jesus had to discern and accept the personal vocation to which the Father called him. The account of his temptation in the desert depicts him specifically and deliberately doing just that by rejecting alternatives proposed by the devil. Jesus had been fasting and praying:

And the tempter came and said to him, "If you are the Son of God, command these stones to become loaves of bread." But he answered, "It is written, 'Man shall not live by bread alone, but by every word that proceeds from the mouth of God.' "

Then the devil took him to the holy city, and set him on the pinnacle of the temple, and said to him, "If you are the Son of God, throw yourself down; for it is written, 'He will give his angels charge of you,' and 'On their hands they will bear you up, lest you strike your foot against a stone.' " Jesus said to him, "Again it is written, 'You shall not tempt the Lord your God.' "

Again, the devil took him to a very high mountain, and showed him all the kingdoms of the world and the glory of them; and he said to him, "All these I will give you, if you will fall down and worship me." Then Jesus said to him, "Begone, Satan! for it is written, 'You shall worship the Lord your God and him only shall you serve.' " (Mt 4:3–10)

No doubt these temptations can be interpreted in a variety of ways, but in the end they all come down to the same thing. They seek to induce Jesus to betray his personal vocation by exploiting his special relationship with the Father for his own ends: the satisfaction of a bodily appetite (stones into bread), the adulation of the crowd as a wonder-worker (casting himself from the temple pinnacle yet emerging unscathed), the exercise of temporal power (the kingdoms of the world). These are temptations to be a messiah in ways the Father did not intend.

At key moments in Jesus' career the temptation returns. When Peter attempts to dissuade him from following the way of humiliation, suffering, and death he has foretold, Jesus lashes out, "Get behind me, Satan! You are a hindrance to me" (Mt 16:23). Again, if we listen carefully, at the very end of his life we can hear the same insinuating, provocative voice that was heard earlier in the desert tempting Jesus on Golgotha: "You who would destroy the temple and build it in three days, save yourself! If you are the Son of God, come down from the cross" (Mt 27:40).

At the same time, it is important to be aware that it isn't just Jesus and a small number of exceptional people who have personal vocations in the New Testament. Every follower of Christ has a special calling from God, a role in the Christian community that is uniquely his or her own. Jesus implies as much when he says, "If any man would come after me, let him deny himself and take up his cross and follow me" (Mk 8:34). The cross here is not something generic, one-size-fits-all, but the particular cross of each individual. Each of us has a personal role to play in carrying on Christ's mission.

This point is clear from the doctrine of the Church as the Mystical Body of Christ, as St. Paul presents it. For example, in the Letter to the Romans:

For as in one body we have many members, and all the members do not have the same function, so we, though many, are one body in Christ, and individually members one of another. Having gifts that differ according to the grace given to us, let us use them: if prophecy, in proportion to our faith; if service, in our serving; he who teaches, in his teaching; he who exhorts, in his exhortation; he who contributes, in liberality; he who gives aid, with zeal; he who does acts of mercy, with cheerfulness. (Rom 12:4–8)

Or, at greater length, the First Letter to the Corinthians, where Paul is at pains to insist that a body "does not consist of one member but of many" and to ask, "If all were a single organ, where would the body be?" Similarly, he points out, in the Body of Christ God has appointed "first apostles, second prophets, third teachers, then workers of miracles, then healers, helpers, administrators, speakers in various kinds of tongues" (1 Cor 12:14, 19, 28).

Here, as elsewhere, Paul is listing charisms — gifts of the Holy Spirit — bestowed upon individuals for use in building up the body of Christ. He stresses that charisms are gifts for serving; and, because there is need for a variety of services within the Christian community, so the Spirit confers a variety of gifts corresponding to the needs.

Probably this wasn't the message every Corinthian was hoping to hear. Some apparently valued the gift of tongues and those who received it above other gifts and their possessors. The dissensions that arose from this controversy led the community to consult Paul. But instead of declaring the superiority of tongues, he asserts the validity of and need for diverse gifts. In fact, he goes further and speaks of "a still more excellent way" (1 Cor 12:31) — the way of charity, by which all gifts and roles and functions should be evaluated (see 1 Cor 13). In this context, Paul concludes that prophecy (inspired teaching), not tongues, is first among the gifts. For "he who speaks in a tongue edifies himself, but he who prophesies edifies the church . . . [and] in church I would rather speak five words with my mind, in order to instruct others, than ten thousand words in a tongue" (1 Cor 14:4, 19).

What is particularly relevant about this for our purposes is Paul's insistence on a variety of roles of service within the community of faith and his stressing that each one is important and necessary in its own way. Every community member has a particular role; everyone is unique and, in a sense, irreplaceable for the accomplishment of God's will.

The First Letter of Peter also makes this point: "As each has received a gift, employ it for one another, as good stewards of God's varied grace" (1 Pt 4:10). These diverse individual roles in the divine drama have been foreseen by God from the very start, so that the Letter to the Ephesians declares us to be "his workmanship, created in Christ Jesus for good works, which God prepared beforehand, that we should walk in them" (Eph 2:10).

Nineteen centuries later, speaking of charisms in a homily on the Holy Spirit, St. Josemaria Escriva, the founder of Opus Dei, sums up the relationship all this has to personal vocation:

> I see all the circumstances of life — those of every individual person's existence as well as, in some way, those of the great cross-roads of history — as so many calls that God makes to men, to bring them face to face with truth, and as occasions that are offered to us Christians, so that we may announce, with our deeds and with our words strengthened by grace, the Spirit to whom we belong.

Around the end of the second century A.D. we find much the same view being taken for granted by the author of the *Epistle to Diognetus*, a work of Christian apologetics that expounds upon the benefits rendered by Christians to the pagan society around them by their presence in it and to it. There is a broadening out here of the understanding of the Christians' role, beyond the building up of the Church emphasized by St. Paul, to apostolate in and to the secular world — the evangelization of culture, we might call it today.

"What the soul is in the body," the *Epistle to Diognetus* famously declares, "that the Christians are in the world." By living their individual lives as God means them to do, Christians raise the tone of pagan society for everyone. This is a tangible, crucially important fruit of personal vocation. But it should not be understood in a utopian way, as if Christians by their efforts could make God's kingdom present here and now; it must be understood in the manner of Christian realism, as doing what one can, in the face of frustration and evil, to realize human goods as much as possible here and now as a way of preparing material for the kingdom of God that is to come. (As we shall see, this is the message of a key point in the teaching of the Second Vatican Council: Pastoral Constitution on the Church in the Modern World, *Gaudium et Spes,* nn. 38–39.)

In its Decree on the Apostolate of Lay People, *Apostolicam Actuositatem,* n. 6, Vatican II makes much the same point as the *Epistle to Diognetus.* The Council speaks of "the very testimony of their Christian life" as a powerful tool in "their apostolate of evangelization and sanctification," while at the same time it insists that authentic apostles be on the lookout for "opportunities to announce Christ by words." And the bishops of the United States, in their stewardship pastoral, place the same emphasis upon the summons to apostolate that is part of the vocation of every member of the Church. At life's end, the pastoral says, "each will be measured by the standard of his or her individual vocation."

> Each has received a different "sum" — a unique mix of talents, opportunities, challenges, weaknesses and strengths, potential modes of service and response — on which the Master expects a return. He will judge individuals according to what they have done with what they were given.

The roots of the idea of personal vocation as a principle of apostolate and service to others go back a long way in the Church. Today, after centuries of eclipse, this seminal insight has begun to re-emerge in Catholic life. But what became of it between the early centuries and now? That takes some explaining.

The Eclipse of Personal Vocation

With its vision of differentiated callings to build up the Body of Christ and of service rendered by Christians to the secular world by the manner in which they lived their lives and carried out their daily duties, the Church in its early centuries was well on the way to developing and teaching the idea of personal vocation. Then the process came to a halt. Complex changes in the Church and society account for what happened. It is beyond the scope of this book to give a detailed account of those changes, but their overall thrust is clear.

The feudal society that took shape in Europe after the Roman Empire collapsed offered most people few options and required that they make comparatively few vocational judgments. Where one lived, the kind of work one did, the religious faith one professed, the authority to which one owed allegiance, and many other large and small aspects of life came to a Christian of the Middle Ages as givens, with few if any alternatives.

Society itself was an intricate fabric knitting together hierarchically structured social roles in complex patterns. In this system an individual's place was determined by circumstances of birth, high or low as that might be. A sense of this social role and the duties and relationships that came with it was central to establishing the contours of most people's lives.

This was true even, or perhaps especially, for members of the upper classes. Their behavior was governed, ideally at least, by what Charles Taylor (in his study *Sources of the Self: The Making of the Modern Identity*) calls "the aristocratic ethic of honour." Taylor explains:

> It involved a strong sense of hierarchy, in which the life of the warrior or ruler, which turned on honour or glory, was incommensurable to that of men of lesser rank, concerned only with life. Willingness to risk life was the constitutive quality of the man of honour. And it was frequently thought that a too great concern with acquisition was incompatible with this higher life. In some societies, engaging in trade was considered a derogation of aristocratic status.

Insofar as the question of vocation was recognized at all in feudal society, it arose almost exclusively for those who felt called to be clergy or religious. The notion that someone could find and live out an unconditional commitment to love and serve God elsewhere than in the priesthood or consecrated life was not easily grasped. Thomas More, for example, faced a serious personal crisis upon reaching the conclusion — after several years of what we now would call vocational discernment that included living in a monastery — that he wasn't called to be a monk. "Since marriage was a mere concession to weakness," More biographer Gerard Wegemer writes,

> it was certainly not a path to perfection — or so held the cultural prejudice of More's age. Therefore, when this young, brilliant, idealistic youth struggled to accept what eventually emerged as a clear call to marriage, he was brought almost to the "very gates of hell." Nonetheless, his humility and legendary integrity led him to become "a chaste husband rather than a licentious priest."

This early conflict, Wegemer adds, "shook [More] to the depths of his soul."

In the case of priests and religious, nevertheless, it seems likely that the idea of vocation was more or less dimly perceived. Even though vocation was not separated from the fact that clerics, monks, and nuns had well-defined social roles within the overall feudal fabric, these roles at least were understood to require personal commitment. The situation as a whole is what one might expect when notions like *self* and *personality* were by no means as clear and strongly emphasized as they are today by the heirs of Descartes and Rousseau, who cultivate a narcissistic focus upon the isolated, autonomous self — people, in other words, like the ones filling the pages of Gail Sheehy's *Passages*.

It is true, as Charles Taylor points out, that as far back as the fourth century St. Augustine in his *Confessions* "introduced the inwardness of radical reflexivity and bequeathed it to the Western tradition of thought." Nevertheless, the sense of the self lay largely undeveloped for many centuries, and only in modern times have people "made a big thing of the first-person standpoint," as Taylor quaintly puts it. Feudal society certainly didn't.

At the same time, we should not imagine that the situation of people in those centuries was less open to moral creativity and human goodness than it was, and we should not suppose that the Church failed her members in some ultimately important way by not proposing the idea of personal vocation to them. All along, after all, the Church taught that God has a providential plan for human life, and that it is up to everyone to receive as God's blessings the good things that come his or her way and to accept every suffering and frustration as the cross he or she must bear. Moreover, to help the faithful shape their lives, the Church provided the sacraments, an extensive body of moral instruction, and the reinforcement of a well-developed religious culture. For the most part, that was enough for simple people with limited personal options living in a hierarchical, highly structured, static society. And the seed of personal vocation at least was present in this setting, now and then flowering in the case of exceptional individuals like a Francis of Assisi or a Catherine of Siena.

But only with the opening-up of society — more fluidity, a heightened sense of personal options, stronger awareness by individuals of the opportunity and the need to find a way of organizing their lives — does the appreciation of personal vocation become a realistic possibility for people in general. And in due course, just such an opening-up occurred. Feudal society gave way to a new form of social structure organized around commerce, focused on commercial centers (cities and towns), and directed by increasingly centralized political authority. The modern economy and nation-state had arrived.

Luther and After

The idea of personal vocation also had arrived. Taylor links the new awareness that emerged amid these momentous changes to the "affirmation of ordinary life" associated with the Reformation. Although this awareness "finds its origin in Judaeo-Christian spirituality," he says, its "particular impetus" in the modern era comes first of all from the Protestant reformers, who insisted that there could be "no such thing as more devoted or less devoted Christians: the personal commitment must be total or it was worthless."

Gustaf Wingren, in a study entitled *Luther on Vocation,* situates the origin of Martin Luther's understanding of personal vocation in an elementary, fundamental fact: "Those who are closest at hand, family and fellow-workers, are given by God: it is one's neighbor whom one is to love." The idea of vocation thus points inescapably to "a world which is not the same for all people. The same course does not fit all circumstances. Each of the social factors arising through the vocational actions of different people has its own character; and the life of society in this way develops in rich variety. . . . Each is to do his own work, without eyeing others or trying to copy them."

"Everyone must tend his own vocation and work," Luther (1483–1546) wrote. And again: "It is God's firm intention that all the saints are to live in the same faith, and be moved and guided by the same Spirit; but in external matters carry out different works." The variegated patterns of individual lives, with their multitude of diverse activities, relationships, places and times, constitute "the instruction of faith, in which all the saints have been taught, each according to his particular vocation." In fact, Luther pushed his conviction of the central importance of personal vocation disturbingly close to individualism in its modern sense: "For occasions of faith are without pattern, let patterns be as many as you please; for in faith there are always new occasions, new situations, new persons. . . . Varying occasions arise . . . and they are occasions that cannot be anticipated by human reason or sense." In these circumstances, "faith is always constrained to prayer. It must walk in desperation and many groanings, then closing its eyes and saying 'Lord, Thou wilt do that which is good.' " Wingren comments: "Instead of seeking help from other people, who counsel repetition and imitation of works that are past and dead, one ought to turn to God in prayer, who can effect new and living works even in difficult situations."

All this was of a piece with Luther's rejection of mediation in the spiritual realm and, along with it, his dissent from central elements of the

Catholic tradition of faith and Christian life. Taylor says faith, as the reformers understood it,

> seemed to require an outright rejection of the Catholic understanding of the sacred, and hence also of the church and its mediating role. . . . Along with the Mass went the whole notion of the sacred in mediaeval Catholicism, the notion that there are special places or times or actions where the power of God is more intensely present and can be approached by humans. . . . The rejection of the sacred and of mediation together led to an enhanced status for (what had formerly been described as) profane life. This came out in the repudiation of the special monastic vocations which had been an integral part of mediaeval Catholicism.

Taylor goes on to trace the idea of personal vocation in Protestantism after Luther, an interesting and important story with which, nevertheless, we are not here concerned. The question for us is how the idea fared in Catholic circles. The answer is complex.

The wholesale repudiation by Luther and his followers of major elements of Catholic belief and practice, and the polemical link they made between this and personal vocation, no doubt help to explain why Catholics were not quicker to embrace the new insight. So does the traditional understanding which Catholics (who accepted it) and Protestants (who violently opposed it) shared: that vocations to priesthood and consecrated life somehow reflected "a hierarchy of nearness to the sacred, with the religious life being higher/closer than the secular." Taylor writes:

> There was an intense consciousness of the dependence of lay people on the life of prayer and renunciation of religious through the mutual mediation of the church, but the reciprocal dependence was lost sight of. The result was a lesser spiritual status for lay life, particularly that of productive labour and the family.

51

Even so, the idea of ordinary life as a calling was not new but old, grounded as it was in "one of the most fundamental insights of the Jewish-Christian-Islamic religious tradition, that God as creator himself affirms life and being." He explains:

> Life in a calling could be a fully Christian life, because it could be seen as participating in this affirmation of God's. In this sense, of course, the Reformers were only drawing the radical consequences from a very old theme in Christendom. It was after all the monks themselves who had pioneered the notion of living the life of prayer in work.

To a degree, then, Catholics were re-connecting with ancient tradition when in time eventually they, too, began not only to speak in vocational terms, but to do so in ways that clearly included the everyday lives of lay women and men as well as the out-of-the-ordinary ways of life of religious and priests.

More than a hint of this appears in that central figure of the Catholic Counter-Reformation, the founder of the Jesuits, St. Ignatius of Loyola (1491–1556). In his famous *Spiritual Exercises,* Ignatius pictures Christ, the eternal King, addressing his summons not only "to all" but also "to each one in particular":

> It is my will to conquer the whole world and all my enemies, and thus to enter into the glory of my Father. Therefore, whoever wishes to join me in this enterprise must be willing to labor with me, that by following me in suffering, he may follow me in glory. (*Spiritual Exercises,* n. 95)

Lest there be any doubt that "all" means all and "each one" means each, Ignatius specifies, in a section of the *Exercises* called "Introduction to Making a Choice of a Way of Life," that in choosing a state of life one should concentrate first on serving God and only secondly on the state itself. He also warns against assuming that priesthood is better than marriage (or vice

52

versa) for a particular individual. Instead, the basis for resolving such questions should be the individual's discernment of God's will.

> I must not subject and fit the end to the means, but the means to the end. Many first choose marriage, which is a means, and secondarily the service of our Lord in marriage, though the service of God is the end. So also others first choose to have benefices [i.e., to receive the income attached to certain clerical positions], and afterwards to serve God in them. . . . As a result, what they ought to seek first, they seek last.
>
> Therefore, my first aim should be to seek to serve God, which is the end, and only after that, if it is more profitable, to have a benefice or marry, for these are means to the end. Nothing must move me to use such means, or to deprive myself of them, save only the service and praise of God our Lord, and the salvation of my soul. (Ibid., n. 169)

Ignatius's point is that the first concern of Christians should be to discern God's plan and will for them (their personal vocations). It is a mistake to start with one's own agenda in place and then attempt to serve God, so far as that can be done, while pursuing one's self-defined agenda.

Anticipations of Personal Vocation

Martin Luther and St. Ignatius of Loyola were men of the sixteenth century. In the seventeenth century we find a clear and surprisingly explicit recognition of personal vocation in the writings of St. Francis de Sales (1567–1622), especially in his *Treatise on the Love of God,* which appeared in 1616.

Francis makes the obvious point that God does not intend that everyone observe the evangelical counsels — chastity, poverty, obedience — "but only such counsels as are suitable according to differences in persons, times, occasions, and abilities." The criterion is charity, which "gives all of them their rank, order, season, and value."

He illustrates this point with a homely example: "When your father or mother actually needs your help in order to live, it is not the time to practice the counsel of retirement to a monastery." Similarly, it is in the interests of their people for hereditary rulers to continue their line; so for such a ruler "the need for so great a good obligates you to beget lawful successors in holy marriage." The point is that the evangelical counsels are given for the good of the Christian people as a whole, "but not for that of each particular Christian. There are circumstances that make them sometimes impossible, sometimes unprofitable, sometimes dangerous, and sometimes harmful to certain men. . . . Charity is the rule and measure for their fulfillment."

There is a tension between Francis's rejection of the elitist fallacy and his conviction, not only that virginity for the sake of the kingdom is in and of itself a higher state than marriage, but that a truly "indifferent heart" invariably will prefer virginity to marriage, as it will prefer serving the poor to serving the rich ("God's will is found in serving both poor and rich, but a little more in service of the poor"). Shortly, though, he clarifies the matter, affirming that "without consideration of anything else, the soul always searches for the place where there is more of God's will." Finally he takes his stand on individual calling: "We would hardly recognize God's good pleasure apart from actual events."

God's special will for each of us settles vocational questions; and it is in the actual circumstances of our lives as we experience them that God manifests his will and we must discern our vocations. "As soon as His divine majesty's good pleasure becomes evident" (when we have conscientiously engaged in vocational discernment) "we must immediately place ourselves under his loving obedience" (we must accept God's will by accepting and living out our vocations as discerned).

First of all, then, an individual needs to see what God wants him or her to do. St. Francis offers a number of suggestions regarding discernment among vocational options.

The practice of stability is one: "If a man is on a good path, let him keep to it. Sometimes it happens that we forsake the good in order to seek the better, and while we leave the one, we do not find the other." The sense of doing the right thing is another confirmation of the rightness of a vocational judgment: "One of the best marks of the goodness of all inspirations and especially the extraordinary is peace and tranquility of heart in those who receive them." Docility and obedience to legitimate authority also are crucial.

> When God sends his inspirations into a man's heart, the first one he gives is that of obedience. . . . A man who says that he is inspired and then refuses to obey his superiors and follow their advice is an impostor. All prophets and preachers inspired by God have always loved the Church, always adhered to her doctrine, and always had her approval. . . . Hence extraordinary missions are diabolical illusions . . . if they are not recognized and approved by pastors on the ordinary mission.

"To sum up," he concludes, "the three best and surest marks of lawful inspiration are perseverance in contrast to inconstancy and levity, peace and gentleness of heart in contrast to disquiet and solicitude, and humble obedience in contrast to obstinacy and extravagance."

There is something refreshingly matter-of-fact about the advice not to devote too much time and energy to the "scrutiny and subtle discussion" of vocational questions, even major ones.

> After we have implored the light of the Holy Spirit, applied our thought to search for His good pleasure, taken counsel with our director and perhaps with two or three other spiritual persons, we must come to a resolution and decision in the name of God. After that we must not call our choice in doubt, but devoutly, peacefully, and firmly keep and sustain it. . . . To act otherwise is a mark of great self-love, or of childishness, weakness, and folly of mind.

Like a great deal else in the writing of St. Francis de Sales, this is the advice of a holy man who understood that sanctity is, along with much else, good sense. He told one of his many correspondents: "I persist always in telling you that you ought to serve God where you are and do what you are doing. . . . If you wish to do well, regard as temptation all that may be suggested to you as to change of place; for, while your mind is elsewhere you can never give your full attention to make progress where you are."

Francis recognizes that, in order to "train us in . . . holy indifference," God frequently inspires generous people to dream great dreams and make idealistic plans — which, nevertheless, God himself does not will to succeed. Does this mean we should "care for nothing and abandon our affairs to the mercy of events"? Not at all. "We must forget nothing of whatever is requisite for bringing the work God has put in our hands to a successful conclusion." But this always is on the condition that "if the outcome is contrary, we will lovingly and peacefully embrace it."

The question of abandonment receives a notably different emphasis in Jean-Pierre de Caussade, S.J., an eighteenth-century French Jesuit spiritual director and spiritual writer, whose best-known work is *Abandonment to Divine Providence.* His thought is relevant to personal vocation especially for the attention he gives to the need to discern God's will in the here-and-now events of life. "If only kings and their ministers, princes of the Church and of the world, priests, soldiers and ordinary people knew how easy it would be for them to become very holy!" he exclaims.

All they need to do is fulfill faithfully the simple duties of Christianity and those called for by their state of life, accept cheerfully all the troubles they meet and submit to God's will in all that they have to do or suffer. . . . This is the true spirituality, which is valid for all times and for everybody. . . . It is the ready acceptance of all that comes to us at each moment of our lives. . . . All our learning should consist of finding out what God has planned for us at each moment.

Adopting the memorable expression "the sacrament of the present moment," De Caussade repeatedly hammers home his theme. And although neither the theme nor his book adds up to a rounded treatment of personal vocation, they do embody some central elements of the idea.

In the nineteenth century, John Henry Newman not only anticipates the idea but works it out at some length. One of his Anglican sermons, "Divine Calls," is particularly worthy of note.

Newman begins by citing the scriptural accounts, noted above, of the call of Samuel and the conversion of Saul. Although different in many ways, he says, they are alike in teaching the need for promptness in responding to God's summons. "If we do obey it, to God be the glory, for He it is works in us. If we do not obey, to ourselves be all the shame, for sin and unbelief work in us."

Among the instances of not obeying — of not generously accepting and carrying out one's vocation — the rich young man whose "great possessions" caused him to draw back from Jesus' call to sell his property, give the proceeds to the poor, and follow him stands out (see Mt 19:16–22); among those who did answer God's call are the apostles of Jesus and the prophet Elisha. The circumstances differ greatly in every case, yet there also are fundamental likenesses in these divine calls: "Their characteristic is this; to require instant obedience, and next to call us we know not to what; to call us on in the darkness. Faith alone can obey them."

At this point Newman notes a possible objection to what he has been saying: "How does this concern us now?" After all, most Christians were "called to serve God in infancy" — they were brought to baptism by their parents, and they have lived since then in a manner more or less consistent with the calling they received at that time; it seems to follow that being called "is not a thing future with us, but a thing past."

Newman concedes that this is "true in a very sufficient sense." In being baptized, one does indeed receive the common Christian vocation. But, he insists, it also is true that what Scripture says about divine callings continues to apply to each one of us at every stage of our lives. Why that is so he explains in a remarkable passage:

> For in truth we are not called once only, but many times; all through our life Christ is calling us. He called us first in Baptism; but afterwards also; whether we obey His voice or not, He graciously calls us still. If we fall from our Baptism, He calls us to

57

repent; if we are striving to fulfil our calling, He calls us on from grace to grace, and from holiness to holiness, while life is given us. Abraham was called from his home, Peter from his nets, Matthew from his office, Elisha from his farm, Nathanael from his retreat; we are all in course of calling, on and on, from one thing to another, having no resting-place, but mounting towards our eternal rest, and obeying one command only to have another put upon us. He calls us again and again, in order to justify us again and again, — and again and again, and more and more, to sanctify and glorify us.

Nevertheless, true and important though it be that Christ calls us here and now, people tend to overlook and even to reject the truth of it, and in this way they risk rejecting his call. "We do not understand that His call is a thing which takes place now. We think it took place in the Apostles' days; but we do not believe in it, we do not look out for it in our own case."

Be that as it may, the evidence is there, all around us, if we will but open our eyes. Not uncommonly, for instance, good people who desire to do God's will suddenly find themselves face to face with religious truths, not previously attended to, that make demands of duty and obedience upon them. (One thinks of Newman himself, who a decade later found himself confronting the truth of the claims of the Roman Catholic Church.) This is typical of how Christ calls us at every stage of life. "There is nothing miraculous or extraordinary in His dealings with us. He works through our natural faculties and circumstances of life. Still what happens to us in providence is in all essential respects what His voice was to those whom He addressed when on earth."

As with them, so with us, divine calls usually come unexpectedly and usually are "indefinite and obscure in their consequences." There is no saying where they will lead.

The accidents and events of life are . . . in their very nature, and as the word accident implies, sudden and unexpected. A man is going on as usual; he comes home one day, and finds a letter, or a message, or a person, whereby a sudden trial comes on him, which, if met religiously, will be the means of advancing him to a higher state of religious excellence.

Newman makes it clear he is not speaking of people who make dramatic changes — what Sheehy called "passages" — in their state of life, occupation, or some other circumstance of a fundamental and constitutive kind; he has in mind people who, externally, remain very much as they were, but who nevertheless hear God's call and respond to it. "Many a man," he writes, "is conscious to himself of having undergone inwardly great changes of view as to what truth is and what happiness."

The process of being called by God and then called again — and again and again, all through life — is God's way of drawing us not only forward but upward: that is to say, perfecting us. The death of friends and relatives is one means; the sudden necessity of making a specific choice, for God or for the world, is another. Unexpected acquaintance with someone whom God uses to bring new truths before us is still another. So are the suddenly acquired ability to resist a particular temptation to which, previously, one habitually succumbed and the newly discovered ambition to serve God more devotedly than before. These are all instances, Newman insists, of divine calls, and we are obliged to respond to them as serious-minded persons. "Earnestness has no time to compare itself with the state of other men; earnestness has too vivid a feeling of its own infirmities to be elated at itself. Earnestness is simply set on doing God's will. It simply says, 'Speak, Lord, for Thy servant heareth,' 'Lord, what will Thou have me to do?' "

We should not exaggerate the importance of the fact that a St. Francis de Sales or a John Henry Newman spoke as he did of personal vocation, as if either of them were giving voice to the consensus view of his time. The point simply is that here and there, from about the sixteenth century on, some Catholic thinkers and saints understood and began to explain this important reality. But the elitist idea that vocation is a calling to state of life and, for all practical purposes, a calling to the priesthood or consecrated life, was dominant.

Yet personal vocation was a fact, whether reflected upon or not. God did go on calling people in individual, unique ways, and some did respond. Some even recognized and embraced their personal vocations more or less consciously and sought consciously to live them out. At the end of this brief overview, we turn to someone who did this in an especially striking way: St. Elizabeth Ann Seton.

Called to Be Mother

Many of the things that Newman speaks of as means used by God to awaken people to their vocations — trials and sorrows, the influence of friends, a growing desire to serve God more perfectly, no matter the cost — belong to the story of Elizabeth Ann Seton, the first person born in the United States to be canonized a saint. Her life was marked by absolute trust in God's goodness, in the face of sufferings and losses of the most painful kind, and by resolute determination to carry out God's particular will for her, no matter what that might entail. As her biographer, Joseph I. Dirvin, C.M., observes, St. Elizabeth Ann Seton's story is in many ways the story of a woman called to be a mother (*Mrs. Seton: Foundress of the American Sisters of Charity*).

Elizabeth — Betty, she was called — was born August 28, 1774, the second daughter of Catherine Bayley and her husband, Richard, a prominent New York physician and medical researcher. Although one grandfather was rector of St. Andrew's Episcopal church on Staten Island, any special form of religious life was far from her thoughts as she grew up. Her interests were parties, boys, and the prospect of marriage.

Even so, she had a gift for contemplation, as appears from her account of a morning in May, 1789, when, alone in the woods, she was suddenly aware that "God was my Father, my all."

> I prayed, sang hymns, cried, laughed, talking to myself of how far He could place me above all sorrow. Then I laid still to enjoy the heavenly peace that came over my soul; and I am sure, in the two hours so enjoyed, grew ten years in the spiritual life.

In due course, Betty happily married William Seton, heir to a prosperous family export-import firm. They had five children.

When her husband's father died, Will Seton took over the business while Betty became a kind of substitute mother to her husband's younger siblings. Though not yet twenty-four, she rose splendidly to the occasion. Dirvin comments on the "fierce" motherliness already so much part of her character.

Although her religious views at this time were, in her biographer's words, a "hodgepodge of belief and observance," Betty was an intensely religious person. An Episcopal clergyman, John Henry Hobart, took her in hand and gave her helpful guidance. She and her sister-in-law and friend Rebecca Seton were so devoted to good works that others referred to them as the "Protestant Sisters of Charity." (This was a time and place when a wax museum on Greenwich Street in New York included among its curiosities the effigy of a nun.)

But Will Seton's health was not good. The tuberculosis from which he suffered grew steadily worse. There were disastrous setbacks to family financial interests in London and Hamburg. Piracy took a fierce toll on Seton merchant ships. The last straw was the foundering of a Seton ship and the loss of its valuable cargo. Will Seton was ruined. His health declining rapidly, he decided on a desperate step, a sea voyage, apparently in the forlorn hope it would help him recover. He, Betty, and their eight-year-old daughter Anna would visit his business associates and friends the Filicchis in the Italian port city of Leghorn (Livorno). Parceling out the other children to family and friends, they sailed from New York on October 2, 1803.

To all appearances, the trip was a disaster. The difficult voyage took seven weeks. Upon arrival, Will was placed in quarantine because he had come from New York, where yellow fever was raging and because he was himself so plainly ill. He died December 27 at the age of thirty-five.

No one reading about these events can help marveling at the kindness of the Filicchi family, who found themselves with unexpected guests, Elizabeth Seton and her daughter, in tragic circumstances. These devout Catholics took a liking to the young Episcopalian widow and began to have hopes of her conversion. Sometimes they took her to Mass. One day, in a monastery church, an English tourist leaned over to Elizabeth at the elevation of the Host and said in a loud, sneering whisper, "This is what they call their *Real Presence.*" She wrote:

> My very heart trembled with shame and sorrow for his unfeeling interruption of their sacred adoration. . . . I bent from him to the pavement, and thought secretly on the word of St. Paul, with starting tears, "They discern not the Lord's Body"; and the next thought was how should they eat and drink their very damnation for not *discerning* it, if indeed it is not *there*? Yet how should it be *there*? And how did *He* breathe my soul in me? And how, and how a hundred other things I know nothing about?
>
> I am a *mother*, so the mother's thought came also. How was my God a little babe in the first stage of His mortal existence *in Mary?* But I lost these thoughts in my babes at home, which I daily long for more and more.

In the spring of 1804, with these stirrings in her heart she sailed back to New York. Although family and friends were aghast when she told them she was thinking of becoming a Catholic, a year later she took that decisive step, to their horror and her own immense relief.

Shunned by people who formerly were close to her, she tried to make a living by running a school, but her first venture failed. To her friend Antonio Filicchi she wrote, "In short, Tonino, they do not know what to do with me, *but God does,* and when his blessed time is come, we shall know." Eventually the pieces of her life started coming together. Convinced she was destined to do some "great work" in the Church, her spiritual advisor, Father William Dubourg, urged her to move to Baltimore. In 1808 she did, opening a school on Paca Street and, with the encouragement of Archbishop John Carroll, taking steps toward the founding of an American branch of the Sisters of Charity. "I shall be the mother of many daughters," she wrote. On March 25, 1809, she professed vows in the Archbishop's presence. Henceforth she was to be Mother Seton.

She and the first members of her community moved to rural Emmitsburg, Maryland, where they opened a school near the recently founded Mount Saint Mary's College. By her wish and at the Archbishop's insistence, her children accompanied her. (One of the Seton girls, Anna, became a novice in the Sisters of Charity, but died from tuberculosis at the age of seventeen, before her first profession. The youngest, Catherine, became a Sister of Mercy and outlived all the other members of her family.)

Life in those beautiful, isolated foothills was not easy, and the little community had internal tensions and problems as well. "I am a mother encompassed by many children, not all equally amiable or congenial," Elizabeth wrote. And on another, particularly difficult occasion: "Here I stand with hands and eyes both lifted to wait the Adorable Will. The only word I have to say to every question is: *I am a mother.* Whatever providence awaits me consistent with that plea, I say Amen to it."

In time, the Sisters of Charity grew in numbers, and their school succeeded; today, Mother Seton's founding of her school in Emmitsburg is generally regarded as the beginning of the parochial school system in the United States. New foundations were launched, and they, too, put down roots. She "accomplished more in twelve years than most people do in a whole lifetime," a biographical sketch remarks.

As she grew older, more and more people looked to her for spiritual advice, including former students who came to see her or wrote her. They, too, were her children. In these years, Father Dirvin says,

> she had come to understand the implications of her position, to realize that it was not by accident that Elizabeth Seton, widow and mother of five children, had founded a religious community, and that, therefore, she must expect the trials and confusion that such an apparent dichotomy would inevitably raise. And when she had found the bridge of reconciliation, she had found the secret of peace.

For Elizabeth Seton, the bridge of reconciliation and secret of peace lay in discerning, accepting, and living out her personal vocation. That is true for all followers of Christ. Certainly, others will not have her unique calling to so rich a motherhood and its consequences, but they will have particular callings of their own, irreplaceable roles, whether exalted or humble in the eyes of the world, in accomplishing God's will and participating in the mission of the Church, which continues Jesus' redemptive work.

A letter written to her friend and spiritual mentor Father Simon Bruté as she lay dying is filled with the ecstatic love and trust in God that came to Elizabeth Ann Seton from wholeheartedly embracing her vocation.

> Mind not my health. Death grins broader in the pot every morning, and I grin at him and I show him his master. Oh, be blessed, blessed, blessed. I see nothing in this world but blue sky and our altars. All the rest is so plainly not to be looked at, but all left to Him, with tears only for sin. We talk now all day long of my death and how it will be just like the rest of the housework. What is it else? What came in the world for? Why in it so long? But this last great eternal end — it seems to me so simple, when I look up at the crucifix simpler still; so that I went to sleep before I made any thanksgiving but *Te Deum* and *Magnificat* after Communion.

Death came on January 4, 1821. On September 14, 1975, Pope Paul VI formally declared to be a saint this woman whom God had called to be *Mother* Seton.

3

THE EMERGENCE OF PERSONAL VOCATION

Increasingly confined by illness to her mother's farm in Milledgeville, Georgia, novelist and short story writer Flannery O'Connor maintained an extensive correspondence whose intellectual and spiritual flights helped her cope with the decline of physical mobility. Her remarkable letters — humorous, earthy, sometimes deeply spiritual — tell of a woman who was gifted but modest, tough-minded but devout, altogether down-to-earth yet endowed with extraordinary gifts of intelligence and insight. Religion and writing were her favorite topics.

In 1963 a letter came from Sister Mariella Gable who asked a question that touched on both: Why was it that O'Connor, a Catholic, wrote about religion-obsessed Protestants and their bizarre doings rather than about her fellow Catholics? The reason, she answered, was that Protestants who have a touch of the prophet "express their belief in diverse kinds of dramatic action which is obvious enough for me to catch." ("I can't write about anything subtle," she explained.) She went on,

> To a lot of Protestants I know, monks and nuns are fanatics, none greater. And to a lot of the monks and nuns I know, my Protestant prophets are fanatics. For my part, I think the only difference between them is that if you are a Catholic and have this intensity of belief you join the convent and are heard from no more; whereas if you are a Protestant and have it, there is no convent for you to join and you go about in the world, getting into all sorts of trouble and

drawing the wrath of people who don't believe anything much at all down on your head. . . . When you leave a man alone with his Bible and the Holy Ghost inspires him, he's going to be a Catholic one way or another, even though he knows nothing about the visible church. His kind of Christianity may not be socially desirable, but it will be real in the sight of God.

Like much that was said about spiritual matters by this writer who disclaimed theological sophistication, the comment is exceptionally acute. Not least, the acuteness resides in her perception of how clericalism distorts the idea of vocation among Catholics.

O'Connor makes essentially two points. First, among Catholics, someone who wants to give suitable expression to his or her "intensity of belief" will be led to "join the convent" (shorthand for: become a religious or a priest). Second, for Catholics, an authentic calling — a vocation — is understood to be a calling to the priesthood or consecrated life.

O'Connor doesn't say whether she personally agrees. Generally speaking, she did not consider passing judgment on such matters part of her job. As one of the most brilliant fiction writers on the mid-twentieth century American literary scene, she was by temperament and training an observer rather than a commentator on what she observed. *Like it or not,* one can imagine her saying, *this is how it is with us Catholics.* And so it was: she got the elitist, clericalist understanding of vocation exactly right. A vocation was a calling to priesthood or consecrated life. Priests and sisters had vocations; lay people didn't.

Here and There, New Thinking

Despite that clericalist understanding, new thinking about vocation began to crop up here and there and put down roots in some Catholic circles. Inevitably, these were ideas that reflected new thinking about the laity as well. Decades earlier, Catholic Action and the liturgical movement had emerged on the Church scene with the message that lay people, too, had active roles to play in the Church's mission and public worship.

Catholic Action was the movement that, starting in the early years of the twentieth century, sought to form and motivate lay people to carry the Church's social doctrine into the secular arena — the world of politics, the professions, labor, academic life, and so on. Looking back from today's perspective, its limitations are clear. Catholic Action repeatedly and officially was defined as the laity's participation in the apostolate of the hierarchy. The implication was that lay people had no apostolate properly their own. Their share in the Church's mission — the apostolate — was a sharing in what belonged to the clerical hierarchy. (There is a counterpart to this kind of thinking in much that gets said and written today about lay ministries, which are widely misunderstood to be the best, even the *only*, form of lay apostolate, but which are correctly understood as forms of participation by lay people in tasks that primarily pertain to the ordained.)

Despite its limitations, nevertheless, Catholic Action was a great thing in its day and marked real progress in the Church's thinking about the laity. Noteworthy, too, was the frequent linking of Catholic Action to the liturgical movement committed to renewing the Church's public worship. An important part of its program was to encourage active lay participation in the Mass.

A good example of that thinking, avant-garde in its day, is found in a 1929 article entitled "Significance of the Liturgical Movement" by Dom Virgil Michel, O.S.B., a leading figure in the liturgical movement in the United States. He points out that underlying the effort to reform the liturgy by increasing the participation of the laity is St. Paul's doctrine of the Mystical Body of Christ.

> All of us together, Christ and we, form a living spiritual body, the Church, the mystical body of which Christ is the Head and we the members. In this living organism, the Church, not all members are alike. . . . The laity are not the clergy, priests are not bishops; yet we are all called to our active share in the life of Christ, that is, in the life of the Church, which is the mystic but real continuation of Christ.

On this basis, Dom Michel declares one of the principal purposes of the liturgical apostolate to be "the unification of the individual and social elements in our spiritual life" along with a "closer bringing together of clergy and people" in worship and social action.

To the question, "How practical is all this?" he replies that there can be "no successful Catholic Action" that is not grounded in the liturgy. Noting that Pope Pius X was widely regarded as the Father of the Liturgical Movement while Pius XI, the pope at the time, was "the Pope of Catholic Action," Dom Virgil writes: "As XI follows X, so Catholic Action is but the further development of the liturgical life," and so "we must have the liturgical life before we can have true Catholic Action." Similarly, in an article written five years later called "Social Aspects of the Liturgy," he stresses that liturgy, properly understood and properly celebrated, is an antidote to "spiritual isolationism" and should lead people to a more perfect carrying-out of their responsibilities in the world.

> The social aspects of the liturgy are . . . counterparts of the natural life of social man. The supernatural builds on and elevates nature. Today the natural social bonds have been disrupted by centuries of individualism. It is not too much to say that the revival of true social human life will be achieved only under the inspiration of the liturgical life, since the specific divine purpose of the latter is to transform human nature after the mind of Christ and to inspire it unto a life replete like His with love of God and man.

Elements of the idea of personal vocation cropped up in other places in American Catholicism in the decades before Vatican Council II. A homely instance can be found in a collection of talks to high school students, published in 1946 with the title *Straight From the Shoulder,* in which an enthusiastic young Chicago priest named Thomas Hosty insists that "we may give our lives back to God either in the single, the religious, or the married state, or as a widow or widower."

Even though they know this is so, generous-hearted people naturally will ask: "What is the highest state in life?" Father Hosty answers:

"Logically, you are expected to say that the religious life is the most perfect, because there is in it less consideration of self and more consideration for others, out of love for God." Then he adds, "But, practically speaking, any one of the various states of life may be the highest for a particular individual, depending upon his or her personal motives and the manner in which the life is lived. Any state of life in which a person becomes a saint must be a perfect state of life for that person." Though not an acknowledgment of personal vocation, this comes encouragingly close, as the writer struggles to break the mold of conventional thinking: that anyone interested in seeking perfect holiness had to do that within the framework of the priesthood or consecrated life. Unfortunately, he immediately adds that an individual's vocation is "a choice each person makes for himself" rather than a calling from God to be discerned by each individual. Still, give young Father Hosty credit for being on the right track.

Another who traveled even farther in the same direction was Father John Hugo. This Pittsburgh priest, considered controversial for his demanding spiritual and ascetical message, was a spiritual advisor to Dorothy Day and the Catholic Worker movement as well as a defender of *Humanae Vitae,* Pope Paul VI's 1968 encyclical reaffirming the immorality of artificial contraception.

In a privately printed work, "This is the Will of God," Father Hugo insisted that all members of the Church are called to sanctity: "It is baptism, not ordination or religious profession, which in the first instance implants in the soul the seed of holiness and imposes the obligation of cultivating this new life." To imagine that lay people "need not become holy, thinking that it is enough to fulfill the minimum requirements of the natural law" is "an error entertained by both religious and lay people, and it causes the gravest spiritual injury to both groups."

Taking as his fundamental premise the reality that the call to holiness is directed to everyone, he at times teeters on the brink of a full-blown understanding of personal vocation, as in this passage from *Your Ways Are Not My Ways* on the need to discern God's will.

Discovering and embracing the will of God are necessary and inevitable steps in loving God. They are at the same time steps in the larger drama of translating into personal action "Thy kingdom come."

"The just shall live by faith" (Gal 3:11). Now it is possible by means of faith to discover God's will, in manifold explicit indications and, further, in all the events of life. Thus we recognize His will and supreme dominion everywhere. Each moment is, as it were, a sacrament — "the sacrament of the present moment" [a reference to De Caussade] — opening up a vision of the divine will, just as a sacrament contains, under humble material appearances, the power and presence of God.

Complementing our quest for God in prayer, we can attain to continual union with Him by looking to His supreme dominion in all actions and events, seeking His will in whatever occurs. As a child waits eagerly for his father to return home, then runs to welcome him with a kiss, so the child of God seeks in faith the Father's will and joyously embraces it in all that he does. . . .

However, it is not to be expected that, because God's will is invariably benign, it is always humanly agreeable. If it were so, we would not need His will to be expressed: Our own will and inclination would be sufficiently divine. (Some seem to think this is actually the way it is.) But doing God's will means "sowing," a dying to self-will, a confidence that God's will alone leads to wisdom and love.

As this suggests, in these decades before Vatican II there were significant stirrings beneath the sometimes bland and stereotyped surfaces of Catholic life. Soon the new thinking would emerge into the full light of day.

The Second Vatican Council

Although it would be claiming too much to say the documents of the Second Vatican Council (1962–65) set out a comprehensive, fully developed treatment of personal vocation, the significance of what Vatican II really did say and do should not be overlooked. For one thing, the idea of personal vocation is clearly and explicitly present. Moreover, the Council provided a body of teaching that encourages — indeed, very nearly requires — its further development.

Two decades after the Council, Pope John Paul II spoke of what it had accomplished for the Church's understanding of personal vocation. In a 1985 apostolic letter, "To the Youth of the World" (*Dilecti Amici*), written for a UN-sponsored International Youth Year, he said that before Vatican II "the concept of 'vocation' was applied first of all to the priesthood and religious life, as if Christ had addressed to the young person his evangelical 'Follow me' only for these cases." But now:

The Council has broadened this way of looking at things. Priestly and religious vocations have kept their particular character and their sacramental and charismatic importance in the life of the People of God. But at the same time the awareness renewed by the Second Vatican Council of the universal sharing of all the baptized in Christ's three-fold prophetic, priestly and kingly mission . . . as also the awareness of the universal vocation to holiness, have led to a realization of the fact that every human life vocation, as a Christian vocation, corresponds to the evangelical call. Christ's "Follow me" makes itself heard on the different paths taken by the disciples and confessors of the divine Redeemer. There are different ways of becoming imitators of Christ — not only by bearing witness to the eschatological Kingdom of truth and love, but also by striving to bring about the transformation of the whole of temporal reality according to the spirit of the gospel. It is at this point that there also begins the apostolate of the laity, which is inseparable from the very essence of the Christian vocation.

Among the points John Paul is making here are: that the lay state is a state-of-life "vocation" just as the priesthood and consecrated life are; that the special vocational responsibility of the Catholic laity as a group is to transform the secular order, the world, in the light of the gospel; and that every member of the Church has a personal vocation, a particular role in God's plan and in the mission of the Church, uniquely his or her own.

Lest there be any uncertainty about whether he really has personal vocation in mind, the Holy Father provides a careful explanation earlier in the same passage concerning how a life vocation is transformed into a Christian vocation. A "life vocation," he explains, is "something which is entrusted by God to an individual as a task." Beyond that, however, wanting to know what God's will is and seeking to know it in prayer, young people who are sincere and good "become convinced that the task assigned to them by God is left completely to their own freedom, and at the same time is determined by various circumstances of an interior and exterior nature. Examining these circumstances, the young person, boy or girl, constructs his or her plan of life and at the same time recognizes this plan as the vocation to which God is calling him or her."

Pope John Paul makes the same link between personal vocation and personal holiness that Vatican Council II makes. In associating holiness and vocation, the Council was challenging the state of affairs so clearly described by Flannery O'Connor in the letter we quoted above: Catholics with "intensity of belief" become priests and religious while the rest muddle through as best they can at a typically low level of fervor and lived faith.

The German Lutheran theologian and pastor Dietrich Bonhoeffer had offered much the same critique of tepid Christians a quarter of a century earlier. In *The Cost of Discipleship,* published in 1937, he remarked that, although monasticism began in the Church as "a living protest against the secularization of Christianity and the cheapening of grace," over time it had the unanticipated and unfortunate result of "limiting the application of the commandments of Jesus to a restricted group of specialists." Reacting against this state of affairs, Martin Luther, a violent foe of monasticism, insisted that "the only way to follow Jesus was by living in the world." In saying this, Bonhoeffer, who was to be executed by the Nazis near the end of World War II for his anti-Hitler activities, was not just engaging in anti-Roman polemics. Protestantism also got things wrong, he observed: "The justification of the sinner in the world degenerated into the justification of sin and the world. Costly grace was turned into cheap grace without discipleship."

So, what were sincere Christians to do now? Dietrich Bonhoeffer was hardly the only one to say such things, and intelligent Catholics were increasingly aware of the problem. But where was the better alternative to Catholic holiness reserved for an elite, which had provoked Luther, or Protestant cheap grace without discipleship?

This was the question the Second Vatican Council undertook to answer in speaking of the universal call to holiness and personal vocation. Of central importance was the insistence that all Christians without exception are called to holiness. In a sense, of course, the Church had always said this by telling people to live in God's love, lead good lives, and so hope to enter into the kingdom — "go to heaven." But the requirements for accomplishing these things ordinarily proposed, especially to lay people, tended to be minimalistic. The unspoken assumption seemed to be that a high degree of spiritual excellence couldn't be expected of ordinary lay people. Just getting by was enough for them.

Vatican II took a very different approach. Chapter V of the Dogmatic Constitution on the Church, *Lumen Gentium,* carries the title "The Universal Call to Holiness in the Church." In a key passage, the Council fathers declared:

> Thus it is evident to everyone, that all the faithful of Christ of whatever rank or status, are called to the fullness of the Christian life and to the perfection of charity; by this holiness as such a more human manner of living is promoted in this earthly society. In order that the faithful may reach this perfection, they must use their strength accordingly as they have received it, as a gift from Christ. They must follow in His footsteps and conform themselves to His image seeking the will of the Father in all things. They must devote themselves with all their being to the glory of God and the service of their neighbor. In this way, the holiness of the People of

God will grow into an abundant harvest of good, as is admirably shown by the life of so many saints in Church history. (n. 40)

There are hints of personal vocation in this, and even more hints in what immediately follows: "The classes and duties of life are many, but holiness is one. . . . Every person must walk unhesitatingly according to his own personal gifts and duties in the path of living faith, which arouses hope and works through charity" (n. 41). *Lumen Gentium* then goes on to speak of bishops, priests, and deacons, of married couples, parents, and single lay people, of workers, the poor, the sick — "all Christ's faithful," it says, "will daily increase in holiness" by cooperating with God's will "whatever be the conditions, duties and circumstances of their lives."

Vatican II refers explicitly to personal vocation in other places. Thus we read that Christian parents must encourage their children "in the vocation which is proper to each of them" (*Lumen Gentium,* n. 11). We are told not to think the evangelical counsels conflict with authentic human development. Instead we are to recognize that, "the counsels, voluntarily undertaken according to each one's personal vocation, contribute a great deal to the purification of heart and spiritual liberty" (*Lumen Gentium,* n. 46). Priests are exhorted to see to it "that the faithful are led individually in the Holy Spirit to a development of their own vocation according to the Gospel" (Decree on the Ministry and Life of Priests, *Presbyterorum Ordinis,* n. 6).

The Pastoral Constitution on the Church in the Modern World, *Gaudium et Spes,* admonishes those who, "knowing that we have here no abiding city . . . think that they may therefore shirk their earthly responsibilities." People who thought that would be forgetting that "by the faith itself they are more obliged than ever to measure up to these duties, each according to his proper vocation" (n. 43). The laity are urged to recall that all members of the Church have their own particular roles in the apostolate — the Church's mission as a whole (see Decree on the Apostolate of the Laity, *Apostolicam Actuositatem,* n. 2) — because each is a member of the Mystical Body who, having received particular gifts, has a unique contribution to make.

The Holy Spirit Who sanctifies the people of God through ministry and the sacraments gives the faithful special gifts also (cf. 1 Cor. 12:7), "allotting them to everyone according as He wills" (1 Cor. 12:11) in order that individuals, administering grace to others just as they have received it, may also be "good stewards of the manifold grace of God" (1 Peter 4:10), to build up the whole body in charity (cf. Eph. 4:16). From the acceptance of these charisms, including those which are more elementary, there arise for each believer the right and duty to use them in the Church and in the world for the good of men and the building up of the Church. (*Apostolicam Actuositatem*, n. 3)

Although the words "personal vocation" do not appear in this passage, it is a precise statement of the idea. Beyond any question, Vatican II embraces the idea and teaches it.

Here and there in the years immediately after the Council the idea continued to appear. For example, in a 1967 encyclical, Pope Paul VI explained: "In the design of God, every man is called upon to develop and fulfill himself, for every life is a vocation." At birth, the Pope pointed out, everyone receives "a set of aptitudes and qualities" which he is meant to develop and perfect, in order to "direct himself toward the destiny intended for him by his Creator. . . . He is responsible for his fulfillment as he is for his salvation." Authentic self-fulfillment, in other words, is not optional; people are fundamentally obliged to "orientate their lives to God" and in this way to achieve a "transcendent humanism" realized through union with Christ (On the Development of Peoples, *Populorum Progressio*, nn. 15–16).

John Paul II and Personal Vocation

Personal vocation is a central element in the teaching of John Paul II. He had developed his thinking on this subject, at least up to a point, long before his election as pope in 1978.

In his book *Love and Responsibility*, first published in Poland in 1960, Karol Wojtyla wrote that vocation, along with its "external, social, and institutional" aspect, has a "personal and psychological" dimension: "In this other meaning the word 'vocation' indicates that *there is a proper course for everyone's development to follow* [his emphasis], a specific way in which he commits his whole life to the service of certain values." And again: "In the light of the gospel it is obvious that every man solves the problem of his vocation in practice above all by adopting a conscious personal attitude towards the supreme demand made on us in the commandment to love."

Against this background, it is not surprising to find a clear, strong statement of the personal vocation theme in John Paul's first encyclical, published in March, 1979. In a passage mentioned earlier, he writes:

> For the whole of the community of the People of God and for each member of it what is in question is not just a specific "social membership"; rather, for each and every one what is essential is a particular "vocation." Indeed, the Church as the People of God is also — according to the teaching of Saint Paul mentioned above, of which Pius XII reminded us in wonderful terms — "Christ's Mystical Body." Membership in that body has for its source a particular call, united with the saving action of grace. Therefore, if we wish to keep in mind this community of the People of God, which is so vast and so extremely differentiated, we must see first and foremost Christ saying in a way to each member of the community: "Follow me." (The Redeemer of Man, *Redemptor Hominis,* n. 21)

Since Vatican Council II, he adds, many initiatives of a "synodal, apostolic and organizational kind" have aimed to put its program into effect. These efforts are necessary and good, but synodal, apostolic and organizational efforts to carry out what the Council prescribed aren't enough. An attempt along these lines "serves true renewal in the Church and helps to bring the authentic light that is Christ insofar as the initiative is based on adequate awareness of the individual Christian's vocation and of responsibility for this singular, unique and unrepeatable grace by which each Christian in the community of the People of God builds up the Body of Christ" (ibid.).

Personal vocation remains a major theme of John Paul II's teaching. On numerous occasions and in a variety of contexts, he has hammered away at the idea that each member of the Church receives a personal calling from God to commit himself or herself to participating in the Church's mission in a particular, unrepeatable manner.

For example, the 1992 apostolic exhortation *Pastores Dabo Vobis* (I Will Give You Shepherds), published after the session of the Synod of Bishops concerned with priestly formation, speaks of the Church's efforts to develop in children, adolescents, and young people "a desire and a will to follow Jesus Christ in a total and attractive way." Obviously the priesthood is one such way; but John Paul II makes it a point to add:

> This educational work, while addressed to the Christian community as such, must also be aimed at the individual person: indeed, God with his call reaches the heart of each individual, and the Spirit, who abides deep within each disciple (cf. 1 Jn 3:24), gives himself to each Christian with different charisms and special signs. Each one, therefore, must be helped to embrace the gift entrusted to him as a completely unique person, and to hear the words which the Spirit of God personally addresses to him. (n. 40)

It hardly needs saying that John Paul II considers priesthood and consecrated life to be privileged ways of following Christ. But he does not think of them as if they were, or very nearly were, the *only* ways of doing that. For him, personal vocation is the key to every Christian's discipleship.

The apostolic exhortation published following the 1987 session of the Synod of Bishops, which was concerned with the laity, contains what is in many respects this Pope's most specific and detailed treatment of personal vocation, including useful guidelines for vocational formation to which we shall refer below. Here we note only a passage on the ecclesial dimension of personal vocation that rules out taking it as an excuse for self-centered individualism:

Being "members" of the Church takes nothing away from the fact that each Christian as an individual is "unique and unrepeatable." On the contrary, this belonging guarantees and fosters the profound sense of that uniqueness and unrepeatability, insofar as these very qualities are the source of variety and richness for the whole Church. Therefore, God calls the individual in Jesus Christ, each one personally by name. In this sense the Lord's words "You go into my vineyard too," directed to the Church as a whole, are specially addressed to each member individually. (On the Vocation and the Mission of the Lay Faithful in the Church and in the World, *Christifideles Laici,* n. 28)

A personal calling from God is not an invitation to pursue individualistic self-fulfillment apart from the needs and interests of others. On the contrary, "Because of each member's unique and unrepeatable character, that is, one's identity and actions as a person, each individual is placed at the service of the growth of the ecclesial community while, at the same time, singularly receiving and sharing in the common richness of all the Church" (ibid.).

We conclude this brief sketch of Pope John Paul's thinking with a beautiful passage from his Message for the Day of Prayer for Vocations in the year 2001. Correctly understood, he remarks, the term vocation embodies "a very good definition of the relationship that God has with every human being," precisely insofar as — in the words of Pope Paul VI quoted above — "every life is a vocation."

[God] weaves with us a marvelous tale of love, unique and irreproducible, and, at the same time, in harmony with all humanity and the entire cosmos. To discover the presence of God in our individual stories, not to feel orphans any longer, but rather to know that we have a Father in whom we can trust completely — this is the great turning-point that transforms our merely human outlook and leads man to understand . . . that he "cannot fully find himself except through a sincere gift of himself" (Pastoral

Constitution on the Church in the Modern World, *Gaudium et Spes*, n. 24). . . . Within the Christian community, each person must discover his or her own personal vocation and respond to it with generosity. Every life is a vocation, and every believer is invited to co-operate in the building up of the Church.

The hope that every member of the Church would learn to cooperate wholeheartedly in building up the Church was a central element of Pope John XXIII's vision in calling the Second Vatican Council. The program for realizing that hope is the teaching on personal vocation — proposed by the Council and fully developed by Pope John Paul II.

And Now: New Thinking Alongside Old

Appreciation of the central place that personal vocation occupies in the lives of Christians and the life of the Church has grown rapidly since 1960. Even so, many people, including many in responsible positions, continue to overlook it. Perhaps they think talk of personal vocation is just pious rhetoric, while, when the chips are down, a vocation is what it's always been — a calling to the priesthood or consecrated life — and vocations in that sense are the ones that *really* matter.

On the positive side, notable instances of the new awareness can be seen in the final document of a congress on vocations to the priesthood and consecrated life in Europe, held in Rome (May 5–10, 1997) under the sponsorship of several Vatican congregations.

New Vocations for a New Europe declares Europe today to be in the grip of an "antivocational culture" whose dominant model of the human person is "man without vocation." In such a climate of indifference, even hostility, to the idea of vocation, young people experience "chronic indecision" when facing open alternatives that, whether the secular culture cares to recognize it or not, are of a vocational nature. These highly mobile young Europeans, with their motor scooters and their backpacks, have become "nomads" of the spirit, who "move around without stopping either at the geographical, affective, cultural, or religious level. They are 'trying out!' "

Weighed down by an overload of information, sensory experience, and material options of every sort, and lacking in spiritual formation, they are like people wandering through their own lives "lost, with few points of reference." The result is poignant and predictable: "They are afraid of their future" and "they experience anxiety in the face of definitive commitments." Although such young people demand "autonomy and independence at all costs," rootlessness itself makes them overly dependent on the values they find in popular culture while pressuring them to seek either the illusion of meaning or escape from the question of meaning in "immediate gratification of the senses . . . what 'I like' . . . what 'makes me feel good.'"

Not surprisingly, *New Vocations for a New Europe* says the Church needs to respond to the antivocational culture by creating a vocational culture in its place. Such a vocation-friendly culture, it says, is based upon values like

> gratitude, openness to the mystery [of the divine call], sense of the incompleteness of the individual and, at the same time, of his openness to the transcendent, readiness to allow oneself to be called by another (or by Another) and be questioned by life, faith in oneself and in others, freedom to be touched by the gift received, by affection, by understanding, by forgiveness, discovering that what is received is always undeserved and exceeds one's just measure, and is the source of responsibility for life.

It is questionable whether this document adequately explains how to create a culture of vocation in the face of the powerful cultural forces opposed to it. But for present purposes, the important thing about *New Vocations for a New Europe* is its strong, clear emphasis upon personal vocation as a necessary element in building such a culture.

> Just as holiness is for all the baptized in Christ, so there exists a specific vocation for every living person; and just as the first is rooted in Baptism, so is the second connected to the simple fact of

existing. The vocation is the providential thought of the Creator for each creature, it is his idea-plan. . . . God the Father wants this to be different and specific for each living person. . . . Vocation is the divine invitation to self-realization according to this image, and is unique-singular-unrepeatable precisely because this image is inexhaustible. Every creature expresses and is called to express a particular aspect of the thought of God.

Granted, this is somewhat confused. "Vocation" in the proper sense includes participation in the apostolate — the Church's mission — and although this is relevant to the baptized, it can hardly be said to apply to non-Christians. What the passage is describing is vocation only in a wider sense — the providential plan God has for every creature — and the *natural* basis of personal vocation, that is, the uniqueness, singularity, and irreplaceability of every human person insofar as each one is "a particular aspect of the thought of God." But even though the passage is not an entirely accurate statement of the idea of personal vocation, it does clearly indicate several essential aspects of it.

New Vocations for a New Europe also makes a crucially important statement about promoting vocations. Vocations promotion should begin in the conviction that every member of the Church without exception has a vocation, and it should seek to promote the vocations of all.

> If at one time vocations promotion referred only or mainly to certain vocations, now it must tend ever more towards the promotion of *all* vocations, because in the Lord's Church, either we grow together or no one grows. . . .
>
> If at one time the objective seemed to be recruitment, and the methodology was propaganda, often with compulsory inroads into the individual's freedom or with episodes of "competition," now it must be made ever clearer that the purpose is the service of giving *to the person*, so that he might be able to discern God's plan for his life for the edification of the Church, and in this recognize and realize his own truth.

This is excellent advice.

But alongside new thinking that attempts, more or less successfully, to integrate the idea of personal vocation into Catholic life, the old, elitist way of thinking remains entrenched in many places. That is hardly surprising considering how long it has been taken for granted; but it is disappointing in light of all that Vatican Council II and Pope John Paul II have said, and in light also of the drop-off of new candidates for priesthood and consecrated life, and the overwhelming evidence that most Catholic lay people, including even many who are serious about living their faith, have no sense of themselves as persons with vocations in any important sense.

It is disappointing that the *Catechism of the Catholic Church*, published in 1992, nowhere speaks of personal vocation. What the *Catechism* does say about vocation concerns only the vocation common to everyone and the various states of life. That teaching is summed up in the *Catechism*'s glossary (numbers refer to relevant paragraphs in the text).

> **VOCATION:** The calling or destiny we have in this life and hereafter. God has created the human person to love and serve him; the fulfillment of this vocation is eternal happiness (1, 358, 1700). Christ calls the faithful to the perfection of holiness (825). The vocation of the laity consists in seeking the kingdom of God by engaging in temporal affairs and directing them according to God's will (898). Priestly and religious vocations are dedicated to the service of the Church as the universal sacrament of salvation (cf. 873; 931).

Some people suppose that the idea of personal vocation is implicitly present in what the *Catechism* says about the vocation of the laity (nn. 897–900). By baptism, these passages declare, lay people are "made sharers in their particular way" in Christ's priestly, prophetic, and kingly office, and "have their own part to play" in the Church's mission. It is the "special vocation" of lay people to strive to influence temporal events according to God's will. They should take "the initiative" in this endeavor. "Individually" as well as in an organized way, they have the right and duty to engage in the apostolate. But although all this is certainly congenial to personal vocation, it falls short of articulating the idea.

Meanwhile there is no need to look very far to find the old thinking still alive and well in official quarters. For instance, a flyer headed "Frequently Asked Questions about Vocations," originating with the Secretariat for Vocations and Priestly Formation of the U.S. bishops' conference, answers a question about parents' role in regard to their children's vocations: "If we truly want to be happy, we will discover how God wants us to use the gifts we have received. Making their children aware of the nature of a vocation, a 'calling' from God, is a crucial first step. After that, it is a matter of inviting, raising the question with their children whether God might be calling them to be a priest, sister, or brother."

It is true that parents' first task in this area (a task many neglect) is to foster in children the awareness that God has a plan for them which they need to discover and make their own. But parents should be taught to help their children listen to God's calling, whatever it might be. Discerning a personal vocation is a complex task, likely to extend over some years for young people. No one can do it for them. Parents should encourage their children to discern what God wants and explain how this is done. They should point out that priesthood and consecrated life are possibilities to consider. But if they imply that the only purpose of discernment is to find out whether God is calling one to be a priest or a religious, parents misrepresent vocation and arbitrarily limit their children's view of God's plan for their lives. We shall say more about this later.

"Frequently Asked Questions about Vocations" also speaks of the parish's role, saying Catholic schools and religious education programs should teach "what types of vocation there are (marriage, priesthood, consecrated life, and single life), and how one makes a good decision (the process of discernment). Beyond the general awareness of vocations, parents, priests and parishioners need to invite, encourage, and nurture vocations to the priesthood and consecrated life."

There are several things wrong with this. Instead of taking note of personal vocation, the reply equates "vocation" with state of life (marriage, priesthood, consecrated life, single life). This statement also fails to make it clear that discernment is a process by which someone prepared to do whatever God wills tries to discover exactly what that is. It further suggests that the specific vocational responsibility of parents, priests, and parishioners is to promote vocations to the priesthood and consecrated life, thus implying that they have no responsibility in regard to the vocations of young parishioners whom God calls to something else. There are indeed things that parishes can and should do about vocations, but this sketch is inadequate, to say the least.

A striking example of the old thinking in somewhat updated form is found in a magazine article "Recruiting Vocations" by Archbishop Roger Schwietz, O.M.I., of Anchorage, Alaska. He was chairman of the U.S. bishops' vocations committee at the time the article appeared in 2001. Here, as so often, "vocations" means state-of-life callings to priesthood and consecrated life. Various approaches are suggested for dealing with the shortage of new candidates (a "multi-faceted recruitment plan" in every diocese and religious order, full-time "vocation directors" actively engaged in recruitment, prayer).

Remarking that "children of every age need to hear about vocations," Archbishop Schwietz writes: "Ten-year-olds know what doctors, police, mechanics and cashiers do. They ought to know what priests and sisters do too. Field trips to the seminary or convent may be in order." There is no suggestion that being doctors, police officers, mechanics, or cashiers might belong to the personal vocations of some of these ten-year-olds; nor is there any indication that children should be taught to think about their future work, outside priesthood and consecrated life, in *vocational* terms — as ways of responding to what God asks of them rather than as means to acquiring money, prestige, and personal gratification; nor is it said that children should be taught to think about their schoolwork and the various issues and problems in their present lives as parts of their vocations here and now.

This concentration on vocations to the priesthood and consecrated life seriously shortchanges the vast majority of Catholics, all of whom have their own personal vocations. Of course it isn't wrong to promote state-of-life vocations to priesthood and consecrated life. But giving *exclusive* emphasis to them errs in at least two important ways.

First, it overlooks — indeed, it fails — people whom God doesn't call to those states of life, and that is a serious pastoral failing (unintended, obviously) in itself. Second, even from the perspective of recruiting new candidates for the priesthood and consecrated life, this approach not only doesn't work well these days but seems likely to become increasingly counterproductive with the passing of time.

Unless young women and men search for their personal vocations, not many will hear a call to priesthood or consecrated life. As the final document of the European vocations congress correctly points out, an inclusive approach is necessary to solve today's "shortage" of priestly and religious vocations. If anything in the present situation of the Church is clear, it is that the old, elitist way of promoting vocations no longer fills seminaries and novitiates. Either the idea of personal vocation will be widely accepted and acted upon, or the vocations crisis will persist, even if the leadership of the Church adopts a band-aid solution at some point in the future such as ordaining older married men (*viri probati* as they are sometimes technically called) for part-time service.

Planning Ahead

One reason for this dire prediction concerns the way that, in the absence of the organizing principle called personal vocation, many good, generous, young people (to say nothing of those who are not especially good or generous) typically go about putting their lives together. Organizing a life is considered a project in which one sets goals, identifies means of achieving them, and then pursues them.

In this scenario, the goals that organize one's life are those that seem to promise maximum personal satisfaction, consistent with one's tastes and abilities. (In fairness, it should be said that for someone who is generous-hearted personal satisfaction may very well involve quite a bit of altruism: helping other people in need, building a better world, even doing something beautiful for God. Even then, though, the fundamental motive remains pleasing oneself.)

People do need a plan for their lives. The trouble with the scenario described above is not the planning but its starting-point. Personal satisfaction is the principle that underlies the setting of goals and the shaping of a strategy for reaching them: What do *I* want to do, how can *I* get the most out of life? But the principle ought to be the vocational imperative of discerning God's will, accepting it wholeheartedly, and doing one's best to live it out.

Even many seminarians proceed in this essentially self-centered way. They regard priestly ordination as a goal to be achieved in order to obtain something they want — being a priest — and assume that, since priesthood is such a noble and important calling, it *must* be what God wants for them. Instead, they should consider ordination a step (*if* in fact they are called to be priests) in the lifelong process of seeing, accepting, and living out God's will.

Of course, not just today's seminarians but people in all times and places have been at risk of substituting what *they* want for God's will. The circumstances of contemporary America, where individualistic self-gratification is held up for admiration and imitation in a book like *Passages*, make this an especially common mistake.

You can hear that mistake, for example, in a secularist intellectual's decisive put-down (as he thought it) of permanent commitment in marriage: "With the average woman in a wealthy country now living about 80 years and the average man about 75 years, how reasonable is it, really, for anyone under the age of 30 or so to make a commitment to be married to somebody for the rest of their lives?" As a matter of fact, it's not reasonable at all, if to be reasonable in this matter requires that one first practice fortune telling. Telling fortunes is not necessary, however, for those who want to discern whether the lifelong commitment of marriage is part of God's plan for them. For such people, as for Jesus, it is enough to see what *God* wants. What *they* want just isn't the issue.

Commitments are large, self-determining choices that last. They do a lot to make us the persons we are, not least because a continuing stream of smaller choices is required to carry them out. Vocational choices that organize our lives (as does a choice of state of life or profession) are commitments. More than being choices to *do* one thing or another, they are far-reaching choices to *be* this or that and to accept the consequences of that choice.

Many human goods remain permanently beyond people's reach unless they make lifelong commitments and faithfully fulfill them. Take marriage. Despite all the shocks and surprises that marriage brings, and all the tempting alternatives to marriage and its burdens, people can only share in the human good of marriage — the rich and profound communion of married life itself — by committing themselves to a partner in marriage until death, then faithfully fulfilling that commitment. The same thing is true of vocations to the priesthood and consecrated life and the human goods that fulfill them.

Called to Have Confidence in God: Walter Ciszek, S.J.

At this point, though, some readers may suspect that, without quite saying so, we are trying to make a case *against* vocations to the priesthood and consecrated life. Otherwise, why all this talk about personal vocation? Why this emphasis on the laity? Partly to head off such misunderstandings, and partly because it powerfully illustrates what we have been saying about commitment, we conclude this chapter with the story of a man God called to the priesthood — Walter J. Ciszek, S.J.

Father Ciszek's remarkable story is well known, at least in outline: how he entered the Soviet Union in mufti after the outbreak of World War II, hoping to serve as a kind of underground priest; how he was arrested and convicted as a spy, and spent years in Siberian prison camps before being allowed to return home. This is a story of courage and endurance in the face of very nearly the worst that a brutal totalitarian regime could do, and it is told with vivid detail in his still-popular book *With God in Russia.*

It is also a story of a personal vocation, discerned, accepted, and lived out in the face of enormous difficulties and with profound trust in God.

87

At the very beginning of his book, not sure the narrative itself will answer the obvious question, "How did you manage to survive?" he writes: "To me, the answer is simple and I can say quite simply: Divine Providence. . . . I don't just mean that God took care of me. I mean that He called me to, prepared me for, then protected me during those years in Siberia. . . . I have experienced His hand at every turning." No one reading his story with the eyes of faith can help but agree.

Born November 4, 1904, Walter Ciszek grew up a tough Polish-American kid in Shenandoah, Pennsylvania. Unsparing in his self-criticism, he recalls: "I was a bully, the leader of a gang, a street fighter." But he had at least two things going for him: good parents and an unshakable loyalty to the Catholic faith that they faithfully practiced and conscientiously handed on. In eighth grade, as much to his surprise as anyone else's, he thought he would be a priest.

First he tried a seminary in Michigan where other boys from his parish had gone. Rising at 4:30, he ran five miles every morning, ate nothing but bread and water one Lent, and swore off meat for a year. When a prefect cautioned him against injuring his health, he replied that he knew what he was doing. "Of course I didn't," he adds. "I just had a fixed idea that I would always do 'the hardest thing.' "

Gradually, the idea of becoming a Jesuit took shape in his mind. He saw many reasons against it, but finally concluded that "since it was so hard, I would do it." In 1928 he entered the Jesuit novitiate. Early in 1929, the master of novices read them a letter from Pope Pius XI inviting applicants for a new center being launched in Rome to prepare priests for work in Russia. "It was almost like a direct call from God. . . . I was fully convinced that Russia was my destination." Immediately after pronouncing his vows as a Jesuit, Walter Ciszek volunteered and was accepted.

He was ordained in Rome in June, 1937, and soon after was sent to a Jesuit mission in Poland. Following the Nazi-Soviet invasion and conquest of Poland in September, 1939, he slipped into Russia and there worked in the Urals as an unskilled laborer and truck driver, celebrating Mass and hearing confessions on the sly. In June, 1941, he was arrested by the Soviet secret police, the NKVD; they had learned he was a Jesuit priest and accused him of being a spy. On his way to Moscow he prayed and thought of the past. "It reminded me of my reasons for being here, of my resolve, no matter what the consequences, to do whatever I did only for God. He would sustain me."

In Moscow Father Ciszek was kept in the notorious Lubianka prison and subjected to frequent interrogations. In July, 1942, he was told that he had been convicted of espionage and sentenced to fifteen years' hard labor. Three years later, in the summer of 1945, he was shipped off to a town in Siberia above the Arctic Circle. When his train pulled in on a day in July, it was snowing.

The next decade was spent in Siberian prison camps, where he did a variety of menial, often back-breaking jobs. Life was hard, brutal, and dangerous. Whenever he could, he celebrated Mass, heard confessions, even gave retreats and spiritual direction. Sometimes he had what amounted to a thriving "parish," sometimes he could do nothing at all.

After Stalin's death in March, 1953, prisoners in the camps revolted. Troops put down the rebellions with much loss of life. Waiting in an open field for what he believed might well be his execution at any moment,

I thought for the last time of my family at home, my friends, my fellow Jesuits, who would never know what happened to me or where I died — out here some place in a clay quarry in the wastes of Siberia. By the time the truck reached us, though, the moment had passed and my reaction had set in: "Do you think God, too, doesn't know where you are? Do you think He has protected you thus far and has now just forgotten about you?" I was immediately flooded with confidence in God's Providence and a strong faith.

Another time, close to a breakdown:

I went up into the hills to look out over the city and make a meditation — a kind of spiritual as well as physical recreation. I needed it badly, because I knew I was beginning to crack under the strain.

I sat for a long time, reflecting on God's Providence and how He had watched over me through all these years. In the quiet, my confidence returned. I could literally feel the tensions draining away, and after a while I lay down to sleep like a trusting child.

On April 22, 1955, Father Walter Ciszek was released from prison. Nevertheless, as a "convicted spy" he remained on a restricted status, was limited in his movements, and was kept under close surveillance by the police. Even so, he now carried on his priestly work openly, despite the complaints and threats of the KGB (the re-named NKVD). Finally, he was allowed to write his sisters in the United States for the first time in fifteen years (they had supposed him dead); the American government intervened on his behalf, and, after many delays and officially-imposed obstacles, he was permitted to leave the Soviet Union. Departing Moscow on the way home, he recalls, "the plane gathered speed. I blessed myself, then turned to the window as we took off. The plane swung up in a big circle; there were the spires of the Kremlin in the distance! Slowly, carefully, I made the sign of the cross over the land I was leaving."

With God in Russia tells the story of Father Ciszek's years in the Soviet Union. But it is in a second book, *He Leadeth Me,* reflecting on that experience and its spiritual meaning, that he speaks most directly about the reality of personal vocation as it is for each one of us.

God has a special purpose, a special love, a special providence for all those he has created. God cares for each of us individually, watches over us, provides for us. The circumstances of each day of our lives, of every moment of every day, are provided for us by him. . . .

[This] means, for example, that every moment of our life has a purpose, that every action of ours, no matter how dull or routine or trivial it may seem in itself, has a dignity and a worth beyond human understanding. No man's life is insignificant in God's sight, nor are his works insignificant — no matter what the world or his neighbors or family or friends may think of them. Yet what a terrible responsibility is here. For it means that no moment can be wasted, no opportunity missed, since each has a purpose in man's life, each has a purpose in God's plan.

4

Personal Vocation:
The Idea in Depth

The story begins like this: "On Friday noon, July the twentieth, 1714, the finest bridge in all Peru broke and precipitated five travelers into the gulf below. This bridge was on the high-road between Lima and Cuzco and hundreds of persons passed over it every day. It had been woven of osier by the Incas more than a century before and visitors to the city were always led out to see it. . . . The bridge seemed to be among the things that last forever; it was unthinkable that it should break."

But it did.

Like travelers plunging into a gulf, readers are plunged into a profound mystery by the opening words of Thornton Wilder's novel *The Bridge of San Luis Rey.* Why were *these* five travelers, only they and no others, crossing the indestructible bridge at the very moment it broke? Is there any meaning in what happened or is it, and all the rest of life as well, without any ultimate meaning?

The Bridge of San Luis Rey, which won the Pulitzer Prize for fiction in 1928, is old-fashioned by the standards of current literary fashions (it has no pornographic passages and takes a fundamentally positive view of human existence). It is a compelling read just the same, and it continues to be enjoyed and pondered by many people.

The mystery at the heart of the tale — why these five? — becomes an obsession for Brother Juniper, a "little red-haired Franciscan from Northern Italy," who witnessed the disaster. "If there were any plan in the universe at all," he reasons, "if there were any pattern in human life, surely it could be discovered mysteriously latent in those lives so suddenly cut off. Either we live by accident and die by accident, or we live by plan and die by plan." As a man of faith, Brother Juniper sets out to seek the plan, the pattern, at work in five persons' lives and, eventually, in their deaths.

His discoveries comprise the bulk of the novel. At the end, sad to say, Juniper's own conclusions are banal: "He thought he saw in the same accident, the wicked visited by destruction and the good called early to Heaven. He thought he saw pride and wealth confounded as an object lesson to the world, and he thought he saw humility crowned and rewarded for the edification of the city." In other words, after mighty labors, Brother Juniper had come up with a theological error similar to the error committed by Job's friends. In both cases, conventional piety loses sight of God's irreducible incomprehensibility.

The Bridge of San Luis Rey is a short book and a superficially simple one, but its speculations on the meaning of life wrestle with weighty issues: predestination, providence, human freedom, the ways of God's love. It also is a story of personal vocation — specifically, the individual vocations that brought five different people to a bridge woven of willow branches at just the moment it broke. People's lives *do* have meaning. Even if they (and we) can't always see it, God can.

No one can live a life that is genuinely fulfilled — a holy life — without consistently striving to do God's will in everything. Whether you think about it or not, striving to do God's will involves trying to discern and accept one's personal vocation and live it out.

It is time for us to lay out the idea of personal vocation systematically and in some depth. We have already said much that follows, but it will be helpful to bring all these aspects of vocation together coherently in one place even at the risk of some repetition.

Choices, Commitments, Faith

All free choices are self-determining: they make us the persons we are. They also are life-determining. They shape our lives, and they do so not only by themselves, but also by predisposing us to further choices and actions consistent with what already has been chosen. That is especially true of the large choices called commitments by which we set out on paths that stretch far into the unseen future: the choice of a major in college, the choice of a career, the choice of whether to marry and whom.

Pope John Paul II speaks of commitments in his 1993 encyclical on moral principles *Veritatis Splendor* (The Splendor of Truth). He writes of "certain choices which 'shape' a person's entire moral life, and which serve as bounds within which other particular everyday choices can be situated and allowed to develop" (n. 65). Someone making a choice like this is setting out on a long-term course of action that will require countless implementing choices before it is done. (On a smaller scale, the same is true even of some less weighty choices like joining a club or taking up a hobby.)

Some moral theologians posit a "fundamental option" for or against God, a complete self-disposal without reference to any specific behavior. They claim this occurs on a level of the self beyond the level of ordinary freedom (and perhaps also beyond conscious reflection and observation). Finding that idea mistaken, Pope John Paul II says the fundamental option of Christian life lies in the freely made "decision of faith" and the "obedience of faith" it gives rise to. Linking this exercise of freedom to vocation, he says: "Jesus' call to 'come, follow me' marks the greatest possible exaltation of human freedom" (ibid., n. 66). Thus the fundamental option of Christian life, the act of faith, is "a genuine choice of freedom" (n. 67).

> By his fundamental choice, man is capable of giving his life direction and of progressing, with the help of grace, toward his end, following God's call. But this capacity is actually exercised in the particular choices of specific actions, through which man deliberately conforms himself to God's will, wisdom and law. It thus needs to be stated that *the so-called fundamental option . . . is always brought into play through conscious and free decisions.* (Ibid.)

As this suggests, the commitment of faith is not itself one choice among others responding to one's personal vocation. Rather, one's act of faith should be the basis for all one's other commitments — one's other large, complex choices of a vocational nature. These commitments provide the grounding and context for all the implementing choices required to carry them out. In this sense, faith is — or, at least, faith *ought* to be — the basic principle organizing and integrating every Christian life. The fundamental struggle of Christian life is the struggle to achieve a steadily increasing degree of integration by setting aside or squeezing out things incompatible with our faith and one's vocational commitments while tying together and shaping more perfectly the elements that remain so that they form a more and more entirely harmonious whole.

Sad to say, in many people's lives there isn't much evidence of this happening. And that isn't just the case with evil, irreligious people but with those who practice their religion and lead generally decent lives, yet whose moral and spiritual growth, having reached a certain level, appear to have stalled at the point where uprightness and a more or less pervasive (venial) sinfulness exist side by side.

These people aren't hypocrites or fools. So, why don't they make spiritual progress?

Apparently the problem is that, even though faith has a place in their lives, it is *only* a place. Faith has been put in a box (perhaps a box of generous size, but nevertheless a box) where it is kept more or less in isolation from everything else. Isolated in this way, faith can hardly serve as the integrating principle that draws other elements together into a coherent whole.

This often is how it is with decent young people who think of religion as involving certain specific obligations — things they have to do, like going to church and avoiding serious sin — but otherwise unrelated to anything else. Since they *are* decent young people, they usually live up to the obligations they recognize, but that's all. Faith has little or no bearing on the rest of their lives.

Young people at least have the excuse that at their age integrating everything with faith is, almost inevitably, an uncompleted task, a project with much work still to be done. That is not an excuse available to older people who have deliberately given faith its place in their lives and kept it there, and who remain unintegrated as a result. The kindest thing to say of them may be that, despite their years, they are morally immature. And, we repeat, all of us probably are still morally immature to some extent. It is a question of degree, of more or less. Good people's life stories are largely about the ceaseless struggle to make it less.

Beyond immaturity, however, lies what can only be called dis-integrity — lives a-swarm with "natural" interests and desires that need curbing lest they lead to sin. In fact, many people in this situation do regularly commit sins; and although these usually are "only" venial, many of these supposedly trivial sins are serious obstacles to spiritual progress. This is especially true if they involve matters that would make them grave sins if those committing them paid enough attention to what they are doing (in the old terminology: if they had "sufficient reflection" to commit mortal sin). Faith may occupy a large place in the lives of such people, but this, too, is only a place and a rather insecure one at that. And much of their lives is lived without reference to faith.

Personal Vocation in Christian Life

Personal vocation is the way out of this bind for people ready to lead holy lives integrated by faith. A personal vocation is not just the calling to make a single commitment — to marriage, consecrated life, or ordained ministry. As its elements are discerned and accepted, a personal vocation leads to a closely-knit pattern of integrated commitments that organize the whole of life in the light of faith through implementing choices.

A few individuals experience sudden, life-altering conversions that change them radically in a flash. St. Paul is an example. But that is not the way for most of us. Even after we make up our minds to begin attempting to lead lives integrated by faith and personal vocation, holdovers from the past remain at work in us and our life situations. (That was true even for St. Paul, who, in Romans, 7:15, candidly admits, "I do not do what I want, but I do the very thing I hate.")

Things from the past — friendships, recreations, interests, and activities of all sorts — may be innocent and good in themselves, but they are not a comfortable fit for the personal vocations and new lives of faith that we now embrace. Either we must find acceptable ways of integrating our old interests and relationships into the new pattern taking shape in our lives or else, very likely with a twinge of regret, we have to bite the bullet and let go of them.

For instance: A newly married woman who regularly spent her vacations mountain climbing with her brother may find that mountain climbing also suits her husband; but if not, she should give up that activity in favor of some alternative that is mutually agreeable to her and her spouse. A priest who enjoyed acting in an amateur theater company when he was a layman may find what he learned by that avocation useful in his ministry; but whether he does or doesn't, he probably will have to give up the theater when he is ordained. To change like this is seldom easy, but growth in holiness requires it.

Personal vocation occupies an important place in the effort to follow Christ, even for people who seldom or never think about personal vocation as such. This is inevitable. For in calling attention to new kinds of acts that need to be performed, following Jesus' way gives rise to new moral norms involving new duties. Among these norms, known only by faith, is the obligation to find, accept, and carry out God's plan for one's Christian life — in other words, to embrace and live one's personal vocation.

Jesus had a personal vocation, a unique role embodying his understanding of the Father's will for him. It was to be a leader whose human life in its totality was humankind's contribution to constituting a new covenant — a new communion of love — between the divine persons and all who would believe the gospel. It is clear from the New Testament that Mary, St. Joseph, and Jesus' early disciples also had personal vocations, unique roles of their own in God's redemptive plan. And so does each of us today.

But being followers of Jesus does not make us his clones, nor is Christian life a grown-up version of the children's game in which players repeat a leader's words and movements as literally as they can. Christians aren't called to go about Palestine preaching, healing the sick, casting out devils, multiplying loaves. For one thing, it's impossible. We *cannot* re-enact Jesus' life. But even if it somehow could be done, it would have no point. Jesus fulfilled his vocation perfectly. He formed the new covenant community; this community exists and he continues to sustain and shape it by his Holy Spirit. There is no need for us to repeat what Jesus has done.

Instead, each of us has something else important to do. Each has a particular set of gifts, opportunities, and other attributes — including weaknesses and strengths — that is uniquely our own. And each of us is obliged to examine that package to determine its potential for communicating God's truth and love, confronting evil (including the evil in ourselves), and dealing rightly with it. This is to say we should examine what we have received for its redemptive potential, much as someone might study a newly inherited parcel of land to determine its best use — growing soybeans, putting up a housing development, whatever it might be. In this way we discover our personal vocations, the particular ways God calls us as unique individuals to help meet the needs of the Church and the world, and cooperate with him in redemption.

At this point, though, readers may be wondering about the case of someone who "misses" his or her personal vocation, for whatever reason — a sinful life, a mistake in judgment, simple ignorance and lack of attention, whatever it might be. We shall take a closer look at this important question in the chapter that follows. Here we note only that anyone who sets out, at whatever stage of life and against the background of whatever prior history, to find God's will for him or her, to embrace it, and to live it out can be certain of finding an authentic, entire, personal vocation.

Personal vocation supplies the context for "vocation" in the sense of state of life (priesthood, consecrated life, marriage, and so forth). We are not meant to select our states of life and then construct our personal vocations within them. Rather, we are to perceive that one or another state of life is a central element of our personal calling from God. It isn't wrong to refer to a state of life as a vocation, and it is good to pray for and encourage vocations to priesthood, consecrated life, and other states of Christian life. But state-of-life callings are part of our personal vocations, *not* the other way around.

In fact, people who don't try to see and accept what God calls them individually to make of their lives are unlikely to see and accept the priesthood or consecrated life — or anything else — as a way of doing God's will. No matter what way of life they select, they will tend to concentrate on setting goals and achieving them in this framework of *their* choosing so as to get what *they* want out of life — which usually means obtaining as much personal satisfaction as they can get.

The commitment of faith is the grounding of personal vocation. All other large life-organizing commitments should be made in such a way as to contribute to the carrying-out of this basic commitment of Christian life. When faith draws other commitments together and makes life an integrated whole, all of the other commitments — marriage, career, and the rest — are made for the sake of living out faith and in harmony with other, already accepted elements of personal vocation. To embrace and live a personal vocation contributes to the glory of God, the building up of the Church, and one's own sanctification. It is one's special way of following Jesus, cooperating with his redemptive work, and making him present in the world.

As such, personal vocation should have a place in the education and formation of children from an early age and especially in the teenage years and young adulthood. (More about this in the next chapter.) The aim shouldn't be to indoctrinate children in the notion that one or another particular state of life or line of work is the only right one for them (and that it would be a terrible mistake if they opted for anything else), but to make it clear that, whatever they might happen to want, God has something definite in mind for them. It is important to help them understand that God has in mind for them a special pattern of cooperation, uniquely theirs, in Christ's redemptive work, and that they ought to discern and embrace what God has in mind, and then faithfully live out their role in his wonderful plan.

The Need to Discern

When we looked at St. Francis de Sales' ideas on personal vocation, we saw that discernment isn't awfully hard for people who go about it with the right attitude and in the right way. After all, God wants us to know and accept his plan for us. We can be confident that he will make the plan known if we truly want to find it and follow it.

Before beginning vocational discernment, however, it is necessary to exclude all morally unacceptable possibilities. Among these is the "passages" model that has no objection to betraying commitments already made — for example, abandoning a spouse for someone new. Nor is there any point trying to discern unless you really want to know what God has in mind.

Faith in Christ and hope for the kingdom provide the essential light and framework for any real discernment. Jesus' revelation makes it clear that God is interested mainly in the kingdom, not in results in this world. We also know from the New Testament that whoever wants the best outcome in the kingdom for himself or herself must serve others unselfishly in the present age. We know, too, that the best services to others really are those that promote their interests in the kingdom, not just their welfare here and now. (Still, their present welfare also should be promoted to the extent possible and certainly may not be ignored or violated on the grounds that only the next life counts.)

Before discerning, people need to make a realistic inventory of the opportunities for service and the threats and challenges they face, along with their own particular gifts and limitations. The next step is to match the opportunities, threats, and challenges against the gifts and limitations. In this way the possibilities between or among which to discern are identified. Other people's advice can be helpful in calling attention to relevant facts — facts about oneself and about the opportunities and challenges — that might otherwise get overlooked.

To get into the proper frame of mind for discerning, it is important to set aside distractions, put priorities and intentions in order, and pray, while avoiding arousing feelings that will bias the process one way or another. St. Ignatius of Loyola's spiritual exercises are meant as preparation for discernment, so a good retreat often can be helpful for someone who needs to discern about something important like marriage, a career decision, or whether to undertake graduate study in this field or that. Often, spiritual direction is part of a retreat. But if it is unavailable or unsound, the advantages of good spiritual direction perhaps can be derived from the counsel of a holy, tough-minded lay relative or friend who has no conflicts of interest and is not hesitant about pointing out self-deceptions and evasions.

Having taken these preparatory steps, one then does the actual discerning. This consists of comparing emotions and observing the harmony and the discord among them.

The process goes like this. Spiritual activities (prayer, worship, spiritual reading, and so on) have aroused a set of emotions that reflect faith and any elements of one's personal vocation that are already in place — Christian emotions, let's call them. Another set of emotions, aroused by careful consideration of the options, concerns the possibilities between or among which one is seeking to discern. The discernment lies in comparing the faith-related emotions with the option-related emotions, which express realities of one's inner, hidden self. If the two sets of emotions clearly harmonize better in regard to one option than another (or others), it can be taken as the option that suits one's Christian self, and it should be recognized as God's will. A sound resolution typically produces feelings of peace and confidence that one will be pleasing God by proceeding in this way.

All this can be illustrated in the case of Stella and Sam, a fictional couple who are discerning whether or not to marry each other.

As serious Christians, Stella and Sam realize that judging whether or not to marry is a matter of vocational discernment. Today, of course, they are more or less unusual in this, since most couples on the way to marriage don't see themselves as trying to discern an important part of their vocation. They are products of what a young woman writing in a Catholic college newspaper calls the "hook-up culture" on campuses today. Angrily she demands, "Why go through the awkward ordeal of a date when we can get drunk and end up in someone's bed anyway?" In a cultural and moral climate like that, vocational discernment may seem as irrelevant as high-buttoned shoes. It's a pity, to say the least.

Stella and Sam, fortunately, have not been corrupted by this culture. In school they were casual friends but no more than that. But their paths began to cross socially several years after getting out of school, and after a while they started to date. Not all dating leads to discerning whether to marry. But the purpose of dating, which makes it not just enjoyable but serious, should be seeking someone with whom to discern about marriage. After a fairly short period of dating, Stella and Sam began asking themselves the same question: "Could he/she be the one?"

Before entering into discernment, however, people who have reached this point need to do something else. They must make certain, if they haven't done so already, that both of them are free to marry and marriage would be a possibility in the reasonably near future. In Stella and Sam's case, there are no obstacles to prevent that, and the conversation that makes up so much of the discernment can begin.

Note that word — conversation. To a great extent, that's what a courtship (the proper name for this kind of discernment) is: an extended conversation between a man and a woman considering the possibility of marrying each other. This is not the place to script the dialogue, but the contents of the conversation are clear enough anyway. Stella and Sam need to get to know each other — not just in a general way, as friends, but precisely as possible wife and husband. They need to address questions like: Is this person someone with whom I'd be able to share my life — happiness and disappointment, sickness and health? Do we both want children and all the joys and burdens they bring? Would I truly love and honor him/her? Could I expect to be loved and honored in return? Are we at odds about important matters of morality and faith? Can I see myself traveling hand-in-hand through life with this person? And underlying all the other questions: Does God want us to marry each other?

Today's secular culture doesn't offer people much guidance in this endeavor. But even without help from that source, the nature of courtship and its purpose point to some basic rules.

One of the most important is: Be honest. Truthful self-disclosure is at the very heart of courtship. This requires that the conversation proceed in a relaxed and natural manner, in a variety of settings and circumstances. The parties should take the time they need to set aside their party manners, speak their minds, disclose themselves as they truly are. There should be complete honesty: no pretending to share interests one doesn't share, no promising to change one's life in ways one doesn't mean to change, no professing to hold views about morals and faith that one doesn't really hold.

Practicalities like money management, budgeting, and lifestyle are relevant topics at this time. But irrelevant inducements to marry — for instance, wealth and social status, offered in an attempt to get the other party to say yes — should have no place, since they are unrelated to what marriage is all about. (Someone might say — though Sam certainly won't — "You will be very rich if you marry me." To which the correct reply, for Stella or anyone else, is, "Perhaps so, and I suppose I'd enjoy that. But marriage isn't about being very rich.")

While the relationship between two people at this point in their lives is by definition a romantic relationship, "romantic" doesn't mean ruled by lust. The standards that apply to everyone outside marriage apply to a couple who are courting. Physical expressions of affection must be brief, prudent, and chaste. Seeking sexual satisfaction is not only wrong in itself but self-defeating, for it derails the process of discernment. Moreover, as happily married people know very well, marriage is much more concerned with a permanent communion of life than with satisfying passing desires for sex.

Like any other vocational discernment, courtship should include prayer that the Holy Spirit will show the way and consultation with others (such as parents, other family members, reliable friends, and trustworthy older people). Sam and Stella readily do both things. Their aim in consulting others isn't to shift the discerning to them, for if ever a couple need to settle something for themselves, surely it is this. The aim is only to get wise, friendly advice, including advice about things they might otherwise overlook or not take sufficiently into account.

There is no hard and fast rule for a courtship's length. The common sense rule of thumb is to take as much time as so serious a commitment requires, but not let it drag on endlessly. Stella and Sam need to bear in mind that, even after doing all they reasonably can be expected to do, they very likely will still have some hesitations. And why not? Sensible people always feel uncertain about the unknown future and are hesitant in taking on serious, long-term obligations. Hesitations like this shouldn't keep them from agreeing to marry. But if either or both have some specific, persistent reason for thinking their marriage would be a mistake, that's a good sign it would. Then they should break off their romantic relationship, while remaining friends.

Stella and Sam come to their conclusion: "Yes. We are as sure as it is possible for us to be that this is what God wants us to do. We fully believe it is our vocation to marry each other." They joyfully and confidently agree to marry, and move on to the next stage: the immediate preparation for marriage called engagement.

Obviously, discerning whether to marry is different from most other processes of discernment in that two people are involved. Still, it isn't unique in this regard. For example, a candidate for the priesthood and a diocese (represented by its bishop or someone he designates) need to discern whether the man should be ordained a priest for that diocese. Complete honesty is required here on the part of all concerned: seminarians and potential seminarians, bishops and vocation directors, seminary personnel.

There are many other instances of joint discerning. But in all cases the question at the heart of authentic discernment is always the same: What does God want?

It is the question of personal vocation.

Marriage: The Discernment Continues

Is there no further need to discern after courtship? Hardly. Discernment is necessary throughout married life. Take the case of two people whom the Church may one day recognize as saints: Luigi and Maria Beltrame Quattrochi.

Luigi (1880–1951) and Maria (1884–1965) were declared Blessed by Pope John Paul on October 21, 2001. From the outside their lives weren't remarkable. He was a lawyer and civil servant in the Italian Inland Rev-

105

enue Department and served on several bank boards. She was a wife and mother, a sometime teacher and writer, who busied herself with religious and humanitarian activities of various sorts. The Quattrochis resided in Rome, raised four children (two became priests, one a nun), and led useful, active lives.

They were married on November 5, 1905, in Rome's Basilica of St. Mary Major. According to an account published at the time of their beatification in *L'Osservatore Romano,* the Vatican newspaper, Maria was the more religious of the two before their marriage, while Luigi, although described as being "exceptionally virtuous, honest and unselfish," nevertheless "did not have a strong faith." Under the influence of his wife, that was to change.

During the next decade they had three children: Filippo, Cesare, and Stefania. Then, toward the end of 1913, Maria became pregnant again. "Because of her difficult pregnancy," the newspaper recounts, "the best gynecologists advised her to have an abortion in order to 'try to save at least the mother.'" Trusting in God, wife and husband said no, and after a pregnancy accompanied by "suffering and anguish," their last child, Enrichetta, was born.

In later years, their children recalled that their parents "led a simple life, like that of many married couples, but always characterized by a sense of the supernatural." Family prayer was a regular part of the household routine, but "there was always time for sports, holidays by the sea and in the mountains. Their house was always open to their numerous friends and those who knocked at the door asking for food."

Luigi was busy with his professional work. Maria was active in the Italian Catholic Women's Association in the establishment of a Catholic university. During the Italian invasion of Ethiopia and later in World War II, she was a Red Cross volunteer. The Quattrochis organized a scouting group for poor children and were active in marriage and family-life movements. In wartime they opened their apartment on the Via Depretis, near St. Mary Major, to give shelter to refugees.

In their forties, they agreed that they were called to complete sexual abstinence within the married state and committed themselves to that.

Other married couples have sometimes done the same, but obviously that way of life is hardly commonplace. In the Quattrochis' case, perhaps its origins can be traced back to Maria's life-threatening pregnancy in 1913. In those days there was no Natural Family Planning, and couples who judged that they should not risk another pregnancy had only one morally acceptable option: to abstain from marital relations until the wife's periods ended. Thus the Quattrochis were morally obliged to abstain. It seems likely that, having accepted the practice of complete continence as part of their vocation and come to terms with it, the couple later agreed to remain continent for ascetic reasons even though the resumption of marital relations could also have been holy for them.

"They were a couple who knew how to love and respect each other in the ups and downs of married and family life," *L'Osservatore Romano* concludes. "They found in the love of God the strength to begin again. They never lost heart despite the negative part of family life — the tragedies of war, two sons as chaplains in the army, the German occupation of Rome — and lived to see the reconstruction of Italy after the war. They moved forward with the grace of God on the way of heroic sanctity in ordinary life."

They did so, we might add, by the continuing discernment and acceptance of their personal vocations, including their commitment to marriage and family.

Detachment for All, Consecrated Life for Some

Everyone needs to set some things aside in order to live out his or her personal vocation. It isn't just a matter of giving up sin and the occasions of sin, which everybody is obliged to give up in any case, but of giving up the pursuit of things good in themselves but not compatible with their particular callings. No one can be and do everything, and in seriously committing themselves to some good things, people must exclude other good things. We think, for example, of the real-life case of a devout young woman who determined that God wanted her to be a wife and mother and, in accepting that calling, ruled out for herself the life of a cloistered religious — a way of life she also recognized as very good.

Detachment is the virtue that underlies this giving up of good things for the sake of other good things to which God calls us. But even a truly detached person can count on feeling some regret at knowing he or she won't personally share in goods that have been forgone. A man who would have enjoyed a trout-fishing vacation in the mountains with his friends may have to force a few smiles when heading to the seashore, family in tow, for his wife and children's sake. A brilliant young woman who opts to study medicine as she believes God wants her to do may feel a twinge of regret about not going to graduate school to become the classics scholar she'd also like to be.

Christian detachment responds to this natural sadness by reminding us that a personal vocation, although in some ways limiting and confining, is part of something much bigger. It is part of what is required for the accomplishment of God's providential plan for the fullness of human life and history as a whole. Moreover, that fulfillment will *never* come about perfectly in this world but *only* in the heavenly kingdom. "My kingship is not of this world," Jesus says (Jn 18:36). This doesn't mean this world should not be taken seriously or that prefigurings and intimations of the kingdom aren't welcome when they come, but only that final fulfillment lies somewhere else. Christian otherworldliness, which values this world highly without valuing it too much, is crucial to the detachment associated with personal vocation.

"If otherworldliness and detachment are as important as you say," some people may be wondering at this point, "then why shouldn't everyone commit himself or herself to a way of life that assigns a premium to these things? In other words — why shouldn't everybody opt for consecrated life?"

A reasonable question. The Church consistently has taught that life according to the counsels — chastity, poverty, obedience — is an objectively superior way of life, by comparison with Christian life in the world. There are at least two reasons for that superiority.

First, unlike Christian life in the world, with its emphasis on goods to be pursued and safeguarded here and now, consecrated life more clearly reflects the communion of God's kingdom and so bears special witness to the gospel. It does this by virginity (or celibacy), which prefigures the perfection of the heavenly marriage of Christ and his Church; by poverty, which points to the time when no need will be unmet and property will be pointless; by obedience, which looks to a communion in which the need to strive after consensus has ended and perfect consensus endlessly reigns. Second, although consecrated life involves hardships and sacrifices, it is relatively uncomplicated and involves fewer temptations; on the whole, it is a comparatively simple way of living a Christian life. Thus, *for those who have the gifts for it,* consecrated life is a superior, simpler way of following Christ — no small advantages over its more common alternatives.

But consecrated life isn't for everyone, and for sincere Christians there are other good ways of life. God's original command to humankind still stands: "Be fruitful and multiply, and fill the earth and subdue it" (Gn 1:28). Christians are supposed to love the world and help perfect it; and although some are called to withdraw from the world, by no means is that true of all. There is no question, as Vatican Council II says, of men being "deterred by the Christian message from building up the world, or impelled to neglect the welfare of their fellows, but that they are rather more stringently bound to do these very things" (Pastoral Constitution on the Church in the Modern World, *Gaudium et Spes,* n. 34). Promoting the human enterprise, working against evil and injustice, striving to restore all things to God in Christ require the presence in the world of active, engaged Christians — namely, lay people.

Besides, the counsels are *counsels,* not commands. They are suggestions to be taken seriously into account in discerning one's vocation. But if, having taking them into account, a Christian does not find in himself or herself the gift for some form of consecrated life, the way of the counsels is not God's way for that person. Superior as this way is in itself, the individual's own vocation — that is to say, God's will for him or her — lies somewhere else.

Living Out Vocations

Though God's invitations are not commands, once we accept them we are not free to renege. Having discerned and accepted elements of God's plan for our lives, we are obliged to carry out our vocational commitments. Pope John Paul II speaks of the duty to do "exactly what we have been called to, what we have personally obliged ourselves to by God's grace, in order to respond to our vocation" (*Redemptor Hominis,* n. 21). We also must accept those many things (sometimes, very important things) over which we have little or no control: our health, the kind of work we have to do, the people we associate with (neighbors, fellow workers, classmates and teachers, even — or especially — family members), and much else. If they are necessary, unavoidable parts of our lives, they are elements of our personal vocations, aspects of God's providential plan for us.

This attitude of comprehensive acceptance of vocation is commended to us by the example of Christ. Think of the incident when Jesus spoke of his coming suffering and death, and Peter, shocked, tried to talk him out of all those hardships. "But turning and seeing his disciples, he rebuked Peter, and said, 'Get behind me, Satan! For you are not on the side of God, but of men' " (Mk 8:33). Jesus knew that suffering and death were part of his personal vocation as redeemer, and he was determined to be faithful to it. Similarly, Father Ciszek could write of his long, miserable stay in Soviet prison camps: "I don't just mean that God took care of me. I mean that He called me to, prepared me for, then protected me during those years in Siberia." Personal vocation again.

We also are obliged to organize our lives in their entirety in a way that supports and contributes to the carrying-out of our vocational commitments. God's plan reaches into every nook and cranny of life. No detail is too small for him, and none should be allowed to stand outside or apart from — much less in opposition to — his plan, as we have come to understand it.

Of course, this statement makes little or no sense if one supposes that vocation means state of life — priesthood, consecrated life, marriage, single life in the world — and no more than that. In that case, quite a bit of one's life can seem to have little or nothing to do with vocation. There will be lots of blank space, lots of time off from vocation — plenty of opportunities for unrelated interests and activities.

Imagine a conscientious married man, call him George, who's in the habit of spending several hours a week golfing with friends. Since he considers his job and his marriage to be his vocation, his only concern about golf is not to let it get in the way of his duties to family and work. (We repeat: he's conscientious.) Provided it doesn't, though, he thinks of golfing simply as time for himself, to do with as he likes.

But suppose George has got hold of the idea of personal vocation and understands that the whole of his life should carry out God's plan for him. Must he give up golf? Perhaps: for he may see that switching to bowling, in a league formed by the families of people with whom he works, would better fit with both his job and his marriage. But not necessarily. Weighing all the circumstances — including those extremely important duties to family and work — he may responsibly come to see golfing in vocational terms: as relaxation and exercise that keep him refreshed and in good health so that he can serve his family and do his job well, as a way of building relationships with friends that provide occasions for him to give witness to his faith and now and then offer a word of helpful advice, even as an opportunity for praising God in his heart for the spirit-lifting sight of well-tended greens and well-hit drives.

A great deal of life is like that. The places we live, our hobbies, vacations, so much else. These things *can* be seen as matters of personal preference, which we are at liberty to settle according to our individual ambitions, aversions, likings and dislikes; in that case, they are viewed in isolation, more or less unrelated to anything else (except to the extent that practical reasons dictate keeping them under control so as not to have a chaotic life). But it also is possible — and it's correct — to view these various aspects of life in the light of personal vocation and to make choices about them on the basis of what will best help us live out the commitment of faith in the service of God and our fellow human beings.

It is important, too, that the process of preparing for something, such as a profession or an occupation, a competition or an athletic event, itself be understood as part of personal vocation, not just a means to an end. This has obvious relevance for students in particular.

For one thing, preparing for a worthwhile activity is a necessary part of being ready for the form of service to which we expect God will eventually call us. And in this sense, of course, preparation is indeed a means to an end. Courses of study and programs of training should be chosen in this light, not because they are less demanding than other available options or promise a bigger payoff in money and prestige down the line.

At the same time, though, preparation itself is part of one's vocation. That was the case with Phil (the law student whose story began this book). He realized that preparing for the practice of law was central to his vocation at the time he was doing it. Unfortunately, not everyone grasps the point. Even intelligent and well-motivated young people — seminarians, serious-minded undergraduates, students in a professional school or graduate program — often think of what they're doing merely as the route leading to a desired destination: "I have to study to pass the test, I have to pass the test to pass the course, I have to pass the course to get my degree and graduate — and *then,* with all that out of the way, I can start living my vocation."

That attitude is understandable but wrong. The preparation, the getting-ready, is here and now a central component of the personal vocations of young people seeking to respond to God's call. That is so even for someone who doesn't attain the goal to which the preparation points. A seminarian should realize that preparing for the priesthood is an important part of his personal vocation whether or not he will eventually be ordained. A pre-med student should realize that her studies are part of her vocation even if she never is admitted to medical school.

Fidelity to Vocation

Beyond accepting our vocations, we must be faithful to them. Fidelity requires putting to work all one's resources — time, talent, intelligence, energy — in fulfilling commitments; it rules out holding something back, keeping something in reserve as it were, either to gratify ourselves in ways unrelated to our vocations or simply to waste our gifts, including the precious gift of time, on idleness or pointless activities like mindless viewing of mindless movies and TV shows.

Plainly, one may never rightly use evil means to carry out vocational responsibilities. For instance: a shop owner or professional person overcharging customers or clients in order to bring in more money for the sake of employees or family; a religious institution's chief finance officer lying to cover up mismanagement and head off donors' wrath; a serious student cheating on an examination he or she didn't have time to study for so as to pass a required course; a prosecutor falsifying evidence in a trial so that a notorious drug dealer will go to jail.

Creativity and innovation are part of the fidelity demanded by a personal vocation. Problems and challenges are sure to come up along the way, together with unexpected opportunities and options — new possibilities for fulfilling commitments of faith and service. But notice that this is creativity and innovation *within* the framework of a personal vocation. That is a far cry from the pattern of behavior praised in Gail Sheehy's *Passages* and regularly practiced by self-seeking persons who shed old commitments for the sake of new ones that hold out the promise of giving them more of whatever it is they currently want.

It is never easy to live a personal vocation wholly, faithfully, and consistently. People may set out full of optimism, but not infrequently this is the optimism that secular humanism breeds — an optimism grounded on false expectations of utopian fulfillment in this world, for oneself and others. When the impossible dream doesn't materialize (as in this world it never will), the temptation to pessimism and cynicism asserts itself. Then yesterday's optimists may grow discouraged, to the point of abandoning the commitments and vocations that seem to have let them down.

The immunization against embitterment like this is Christian hope. Unlike secular optimism, hope takes a realistic view of evil and the limitations of what can be accomplished in this world. It looks ultimately to God, rather than to human intelligence and will, for the final victory over evil and complete and lasting fulfillment — for oneself and everyone and everything else. Hope provides the strength to persevere faithfully in a vocation in the face of a painful situation — poor health, a frustrating job, a diocese or religious order or school that has become dysfunctional, an unsatisfactory marriage, difficult and disappointing children, and so much else. Hope makes it possible to accept the painful things that can't be changed as elements in God's plan for us.

From our perspective, of course, the stories of our lives and the histories of our communities — families, nation, world, and Church — don't always make good sense. Clever editing may tidy them up, but at bottom the raw material remains an incoherent jumble whose loose ends and suffering seem pointless. Where is God's providential plan being realized in all this?

Part of the answer concerns the fact that struggle and pain usually are required for the realization of what is most noble about human beings. A championship sports team, to take a simple example, must work hard and struggle against adversity, and its excellence is all the greater if it went into its last match as underdog and came from behind to win. Similarly, Jesus as a human being couldn't have become who he is now, the risen and glorified Lord, without living as he lived, suffering as he suffered, and dying as he died. God allows us also to encounter challenges, and those who are favored often must suffer greatly.

But there is more to the answer than that. Vatican Council II teaches (in the Pastoral Constitution on the Church in the Modern World, *Gaudium et Spes,* n. 38, translation ours) that the Holy Spirit calls some Christians "to dedicate themselves to the earthly service of human persons, and by this ministry of theirs to prepare material for the heavenly kingdom." Then it goes on to deal with the ultimate significance of human action in this life, including how the pursuit of human goods in the present age can contribute to the everlasting kingdom that is to come:

> For after we have promoted on earth, in the Spirit of the Lord and in accord with his command, the goods of human dignity, familial communion, and freedom — that is to say, all the good fruits of our nature and effort — then we shall find them once more, but cleansed of all dirt, lit up, and transformed, when Christ gives back to the Father an eternal and universal kingdom: "a kingdom of truth and life, a kingdom of holiness and grace, a kingdom of justice, love, and peace." (n. 39, translation ours)

Since all good fruits of human nature and effort will be found again in the kingdom, the teaching must be extended beyond saying *some* will prepare material for the kingdom to make the point that *every* Christian prepares material for the kingdom whenever he or she does anything in the Spirit of the Lord and according to his will. All Christians who enter the kingdom will find there once more all the good fruits of their Christian lives — but freed of sin and imperfection, transformed, and reworked into the fabric of heavenly glory.

The realization of God's plan will be obvious to those who reach their heavenly home, just as the realization of an architect's plan for a beautiful cathedral is obvious to people entering the completed edifice. But God's plan also is already being realized in our lives on earth, even though that often doesn't seem to be so, just as the architect's plan is being realized even while materials for the cathedral are being piled up on a nearby lot. Someone who keeps looking at the lot while the construction is going on, in hopes of seeing a cathedral emerge, is bound to be disappointed; yet everything on the lot here and now is just as it should be. And, similarly, the providential organization of our lives on earth for the sake of preparing materials for the kingdom is perfectly coherent, though it may not look so to us.

The first of the materials we are preparing is ourselves, as individuals and as communities of persons. Life shapes us into who we are to be; and it isn't reasonable to expect either our individual lives or human history gradually to take on the appearance of heavenly glory. Someone who grasps this can embrace his or her present life with enthusiasm, despite the loose ends and the pain; and the expectation of finding again in the kingdom all the good fruits of what now is done gives the present life a depth, a density of significance, lacking if one focuses only on the important but partial truth that this life is a pilgrimage and this world is passing away.

Jesus' Vocation and Ours: Redemption and Co-Redemption

We repeat: Jesus had a personal vocation, a vocation uniquely his as a man. It is important to our living as Christians that we not emphasize Jesus' divine nature (his being God) so one-sidedly as to neglect or de-emphasize the reality of his human nature (his being man, with a genuine human life). Central to it was the discerning, accepting, and faithful living-out of the Father's will for him — his vocation.

Jesus' unique vocation was to be savior, redeemer, to restore the broken relationship between God and human beings by establishing a new covenant into which others could enter by believing in him and undertaking to follow him. This following of Christ essentially means joining and cooperating with his covenant-forming, redemptive action.

It has various aspects: accepting the gospel message, making the commitment of faith, receiving baptism, participating in the Eucharist and being a member of the Church — the community of Christ's followers formed and sustained by the Eucharist. But another aspect has particular relevance here: discerning, accepting, and faithfully living out our vocations, which in their splendid diversity are all of them ways of cooperating with Jesus in his redemptive work.

In a certain sense, then, the personal vocation of every follower of Jesus is to co-redeem with him. To be sure, Jesus' redeeming activity — his perfect fulfillment of the Father's will — was entirely sufficient to accomplish *its* purpose; it is not as if our participation were needed to make up some defect or deficiency in what he did. At the same time, however, each of us has a unique contribution to make in *continuing* Jesus' work in our own lives and in today's world.

St. Paul got to the heart of this profound reality in the case of suffering. Writing to the Christians in a town in the northwest corner of Asia Minor called Colossae, he said: "Now I rejoice in my sufferings for your sake, and in my flesh I complete what is lacking in Christ's afflictions for the sake of his body, that is, the church, of which I became a minister according to the divine office which was given to me for you, to make the word of God fully known" (Col 1:24–25). One is reminded of something St. Josemaria Escriva said: "You have come at a good time to take up the Cross. The redemption is taking place — now! — and Jesus needs many Simons of Cyrene."

But participation in Christ's redemptive work doesn't end with the experience of suffering. Jesus is prepared to use the totality of our lives — all our individual gifts and circumstances, relationships, joys and sorrows and strivings — to carry on his redemptive work here and now. And he wants to do it with our cooperation.

We make our contribution by integrating our activities and our lives in the service of others according to God's plan as it is discerned in our unique vocations. And we do it, or at least we *ought* to do it, in the present circumstances of our lives, even though these circumstances may include the enforced passivity of ill health, frustration and failure in work or family life or apostolic undertakings, or simply the fact that we are presently preparing to do something in the future that we are tempted to think of as our *real* purpose in life, our *real* vocation.

Vocation and Holiness

Finally, a word about personal vocation and holiness.

In baptism, people who wish to follow Jesus reject sin, seek and accept faith, and promise to follow Christ — in other words, they promise to abide in and increasingly integrate into their lives the faith, hope, and love which the Holy Spirit gives in this sacrament. In confirmation, they receive the Holy Spirit to enlighten and strengthen them for courageous, faithful witnessing to the gospel — in other words, they receive the Spirit so as to carry on Jesus' mission by making his kingdom more visible in the world and more available to others. In the Eucharist, they unite themselves with Jesus' redemptive act, his self-gift to the Father, and enter into fully personal, bodily unity with Jesus and one another in the resurrection life that will last forever.

Fully to enjoy the benefits of baptism, confirmation, and the Eucharist for themselves and others, Jesus' followers must organize their lives around these three sacraments. This, too, requires discerning, accepting, and faithfully carrying out our personal vocations. Of course, a holy life also requires devout and regular reception of the sacrament of penance and appropriate, regular personal prayer and devotion. So people who live out their personal vocations and satisfy the common requirements of religious observance fulfill all their Christian responsibilities; and in doing this they live prophetic, kingly, and priestly lives modeled on Christ's life.

Such people fulfill their prophetic responsibilities. They attend to God's word and try to understand it — doing that is part of their praying. By putting faith into action through works of service and through resignation to their sufferings, their lives bear witness; and in virtue of their meditating on God's word and their prayer, they are ready to complement their witness of life by giving an account of the hope that is in them (see 1 Pt 3:15). Thus the sacrament of confirmation is fruitful in their lives, with great benefits both for themselves and for those to whom they bear witness.

Such people fulfill their kingly responsibilities. They gradually overcome sin in themselves and encourage others to do the same. Although their lives are unavoidably limited in their good effects, they do promote good and reduce the evil in the world. Because the kingdom is the ultimate end of all they do, love of God and neighbor informs their hope and faith. And because of this consistent and stable purpose in life, their good actions gradually integrate all of their feelings with their faith, hope, and love. But this is holiness. So the sacrament of baptism bears its fruit in God's children whose lives glorify their heavenly Father.

Such people fulfill their priestly responsibilities when they participate in the Eucharist. Then, together with Jesus' self-sacrifice, they offer as sacrifices not only themselves but the communions of persons they forge with others, along with all the other good fruits of their nature and effort (see *Gaudium et Spes,* n. 39). These sacrifices are materials that will be transformed in Jesus' recapitulation, or restoration, of all creation. They will be found again in the kingdom. Thus the sacrament of the Eucharist bears its fruit of sustaining and nurturing the communion of Christians with the risen Lord and, in him, not only with one another but with the Father and the Holy Spirit.

Understood correctly and lived wholeheartedly, our personal vocations vastly enrich our lives, adding dimensions of significance life could have in no other way. There is no such thing as an unimportant vocation, for every personal vocation not only is a calling from God, but a unique, irreplaceable way of cooperating with Jesus Christ in his redemptive work.

Vocational Commitment: The Example of the Intellectual Life

We saw the important role of commitments above. These large context-establishing choices go far to organize our lives — not only because they set us on particular paths but especially because following the path one has accepted will require innumerable implementing choices. This is especially clear in the case of commitments of an overtly vocational kind, such as a state of life or occupation. Commitments like this correspond to Pope John Paul II's description of choices that "'shape' a person's entire moral life, and which serve as bounds within which other particular everyday choices can be situated and allowed to develop" (The Splendor of Truth, *Veritatis Splendor,* n. 65).

A commitment to the intellectual life is a good example of what we mean, although certainly not the only one.

The French Dominican theologian A. G. Sertillanges points out (in a book called *The Intellectual Life*) that the "intellectual vocation" is a true vocation "written in our instincts, in our powers, in a sort of inner impulse of which reason must judge." As a vocation, it is "something that cannot be had for the asking. It comes from heaven and from our first nature. The whole point is to be docile to God and to oneself as soon as they have spoken."

Thus a calling to the life of the mind is not to be taken lightly. It is not for dilettantes. "A vocation is not fulfilled by vague reading and a few scattered writings. It requires penetration and continuity and methodical effort, so as to attain a fullness of development which will correspond to the call of the Spirit, and to the resources that it has pleased Him to bestow on us." A true calling to this way of life has something of the sacred about it. It carries momentous consequences: "All roads but one are bad roads for you, since they diverge from the direction in which your action is expected and required. Do not prove faithless to God, to your brethren and to yourself by rejecting a sacred call."

A serious commitment to the intellectual life can take many forms, but teaching is probably the most familiar. In a paper called "The Vocation of a Catholic Teacher/Scholar," American theologian William E. May speaks of three "prior principles" that underlie it.

First, the unity of all truth. The Catholic teacher and scholar comes to his or her occupation convinced, in the light of faith, of the truth and enormous importance of certain fundamental facts. Some of these can be known by human reason without special help, for example, that human persons are superior in kind to all other animals and shape their lives and their selves by free choices. Others have been revealed by God, such as the wounding of human nature by sin, redemption by Christ, and the possibility of sharing in God's life by grace. To be certain about things like these does not preempt honest inquiry but encourages it, in the spirit of faith seeking understanding.

Second, fidelity to the Magisterium or teaching authority of the Church, which is vested in the pope and the bishops. This fidelity is grounded in the conviction that the Church was founded by Christ to sanctify and teach — that is, essentially, to continue the work of Jesus, and not just to do these things in his name (as a woman might be said to carry on the tradition of a revered mentor who taught her to play a musical instrument), but under the guidance and protection he provides through his Holy Spirit. The Catholic teacher and scholar accepts what the pope and bishops propose as the content of the Church's faith not because popes and bishops are smarter or better than everyone else, but because the Lord Jesus teaches through them.

Third, dedication of the intelligence to Christ's service. Piety is necessary but not sufficient. Catholic teachers and scholars must be good at what they do — good enough for it to be worth dedicating to Christ. As Father Sertillanges points out, discipline and hard work according to the profession's highest standards are essential. A Catholic does this not just as any serious-minded and conscientious professional would, but precisely as someone does it who sees using the intellect in vocational terms — as participating in Jesus' redemptive work, as conforming the life of the mind to its origin and end, who is God.

May goes on to describe the work of the teacher and scholar as involving preparation, classroom presentation, correcting papers and examinations, relations with students, research and publication. Obviously, any conscientious teacher shares these same duties, but they have special meaning for one who understands them as elements of personal vocation and specific ways of carrying out a vocational commitment to the intellectual life.

The specifics of other vocational commitments will be different, but the underlying pattern will be the same. Something that May says of the teacher and scholar might be said of anyone working in any field: "Only by sanctifying this work, sanctifying himself in it, and sanctifying others through it will he be faithful to his baptismal commitment and become fully the being his Father wills him to be."

A Knight of Truth

The twentieth-century French philosopher Jacques Maritain is a striking instance of someone who discerned, accepted, and lived out in just this spirit a personal vocation that included a commitment to the life of scholarship.

Maritain (1882–1973) was born in Paris and studied at the Sorbonne and at Heidelberg. He converted to Catholicism when he was twenty-four. He lectured widely in Europe and the United States on the philosophy of St. Thomas Aquinas and held chairs at the Institut Catholique in Paris (1914–1933), the Institute for Medieval Studies in Toronto (1933–1945), and Princeton University (1948–1952). He was French Ambassador to the Holy See from 1945 to 1948.

The author of some sixty books (among them *The Degrees of Knowledge, Creative Intuition in Art and Poetry,* and *Integral Humanism*), Maritain was an important influence on the thinking of Pope Paul VI and, through him, on the Second Vatican Council. Especially noteworthy were Maritain's vision of Christian humanism and of the role Christians should play in shaping the secular order. It's said Pope Paul gave serious consideration to naming him a lay cardinal, but Maritain declined the honor.

Following Vatican II, Jacques Maritain became disgusted with the defections and dissent that marred the postconciliar years, and with the adoption by some Catholics of false secularist values. He skewered the latter error as "kneeling to the world" in a sharp-eyed, sharp-tongued book called *The Peasant of the Garonne*. His wife Raissa died in 1960, and Maritain spent the last years of his life residing with the Little Brothers of Jesus in Toulouse, France, eventually becoming a Brother himself.

His vocational trajectory is traced in two books of memoirs by Raissa Maritain. *We Have Been Friends Together* and *Adventures in Grace* give a moving portrait of this remarkable couple and their remarkable intellectual and spiritual lives.

They met as students at the Sorbonne. He was the son of wealthy Protestants, she the daughter of Russian Jews. Both were brilliant, earnest, lacking religious faith yet desperate for something to believe. But not if finding it took too long. Jacques and Raissa agreed that they would be patient for a while, hoping "the meaning of life would reveal itself"; but "if the experiment should not be successful, the solution would be suicide; suicide before the years had accumulated their dust, before our youthful strength was spent. We wanted to die by a free act if it were impossible to live according to the truth."

They were rescued — up to a point — by the *élan vital* philosophy Henri Bergson had developed in opposition to the prevailing positivism of the day. In time, the Maritains would break decisively with Bergson's thought, but for the moment his ideas offered refuge and relief. Convinced they were meant to pursue truth together, they married in 1904.

Then something new appeared on their horizon. Under the influence of the ardently Catholic writer Leon Bloy, they were led to Catholicism, and in 1906 the Maritains entered the Church. Two years later, guided by a Dominican priest, Raissa discovered the writings of St. Thomas Aquinas. She told Jacques of her find, but, preoccupied with his work, he let a year go by before looking into the writings of the great thirteenth-century thinker. Astonished by their brilliance and insight, he plunged into the study of Aquinas's thought.

Earlier, Maritain had passed up an academic career in state schools because he would not have been allowed to teach the truth there as he had come to see it. Now he and Raissa saw that they were called to foster the right relationship between reason and faith. "We felt," she writes, "that to implant reason in faith . . . does not weaken reason but strengthens it, does not enslave it but frees it, does not denature it but restores it to the purity of its true nature."

The first public result of Jacques' immersion in Aquinas was a series of lectures delivered in April and May of 1913 at the Institut Catholique. Their critique of Bergson's philosophy, which had begun to infect even Catholic thought, caused a sensation. Raissa calls these lectures "the first manifesto of the Thomistic renaissance in France." Maritain had discovered his vocation. He was to be, as his wife expresses it, "a knight of truth." In the introduction to a book on Bergson he wrote: "God does not need our services, and yet He wishes us to serve Him." This Jacques Maritain set out consciously to do.

The decades that followed were filled with activity — teaching, writing, travel, important work in the service of the French state and the Church. It was central to his vocation, Raissa says, "to bring to light the vital forces of Thomism, to carry the light of this great doctrine to all the problems of our times, . . . to reinsert it into the existential reality of the movement of culture and philosophy."

Considered from this perspective, it is painfully ironic that the Thomistic tradition has been abandoned — repudiated even — by many members of the Catholic academic and intellectual elite in the last thirty-five years (more kneeling to the world, it appears). Thomism, however, is a philosophy with enormous internal resources and resiliency. It has experienced periods of relative neglect before, and it can be expected to survive this one, too.

And academic fashions of the moment take nothing away from either the purity of Jacques Maritain's vocational vision or the intensity of his commitment in embracing it. As Raissa Maritain says:

Bossuet reproached Descartes with having too greatly feared the Church; Jacques has not feared her, he has loved her and given himself to her with absolute trust. . . . The more he has lived, the deeper have become his love of the Church and his consciousness of belonging to the Mystical Body of Christ. And at the same time, his freedom has grown greater, and he has better understood his vocation as a philosopher engaged in the drama of the profane world and temporal civilization.

In *The Peasant of the Garonne,* Maritain himself remarks:

> After all, a Christian can be a philosopher. And if he believes that, in order to philosophize, he should lock his faith up in a strongbox — that is, should cease being a Christian while he philosophizes — he is maiming himself, which is no good (all the more as philosophizing takes up the better part of his time). He is also deluding himself, for these kinds of strongboxes have always poor locks. But if, while he philosophizes, he does not shut his faith up in a strongbox, he is philosophizing in faith, willy-nilly. It is better that he should be aware of it.

Thomas Aquinas would have approved.

5

PUTTING THE IDEA TO WORK

God has in mind for each of us a unique life of good works to be lived according to his plan. Its name is personal vocation. The Letter to the Ephesians 2:10 contains a clear statement of the idea, with different translations shedding light on different aspects.

The RSV translation says we are God's "workmanship, created in Christ Jesus for good works, which God prepared beforehand, that we should walk in them." The Jerusalem Bible suggests another nuance by calling us "God's work of art" and saying we are "created in Christ Jesus to live the good life as from the beginning he had meant us to live it." Ronald Knox's version may be clearest of all concerning the idea we are considering: "We are his design; God has created us in Christ Jesus, pledged to such good actions as he has prepared beforehand, to be the employment of our lives."

Although each life of good works is different from every other, all have certain features in common. Unique though it is, each personal vocation is God's plan for the use to be made by a particular individual, within all the circumstances of life, of the special gifts God has given him or her — gifts meant to be used to serve others and prepare materials for the kingdom.

Vatican Council II says God has made the faithful free "so that — having set aside self-love and taken up and humanized all earthly forces — they can reach out toward that future when humanity itself will become an offering accepted by God" (Pastoral Constitution on the Church in the Modern World, *Gaudium et Spes,* n. 38, our translation). There is no *reasonable* alternative to this use of freedom, and the only *rational* alternative to it is to identify goals and objectives for oneself — things one wants to get out of life — and then pursue them by calculation and well-crafted action.

Personal vocation ought properly to be a central theme of moral theology, yet classical moral theologians almost entirely overlooked it, as have most moral theologians since Vatican II. These latter generally have continued in the legalistic tradition by drawing lines between what is obligatory and what isn't, then lightening people's burdens (as they suppose) by suggesting that whatever is not strictly obligatory can safely be ignored. In a system like this, moral norms are treated as rules rather than truths, while manipulative efforts to get the good things God promises by playing by the rules take the place of grateful commitment to doing God's will.

But aren't virtues what really count? Isn't it a lot more important (and much less chancy) to live a life organized by the good habits called virtues than to try to live out this undefined, subjective something called a personal vocation, by definition significantly different for every individual?

History helps answer these questions. Virtues were especially important in Aristotle's thinking. He knew nothing of original sin and did not understand free choice. Faced with the need to account for human behavior that so often fell short of human capacities, Aristotle turned to the model of the inadequate skills of people who are immature, mentally defective, badly taught, or culturally deprived. As the remedy for unskillful performance is the training and practice by which skills are developed, so the remedy for wrongful behavior lay in developing habits of excellent behavior — virtues.

Rightly wishing to avoid a legalistic emphasis on rules, St. Thomas Aquinas drew heavily on Aristotle's thinking about virtue. Though he amended that thinking, he overlooked personal vocation, and many of his followers today mistakenly suppose that living by virtues is the only alternative to living by rules. In one sense, of course, that is true. Only people who have acquired virtues are in a position to forget about rules. But rules are necessary for people who wish to do the right thing yet lack mature virtues. Still, rules by themselves are inadequate, because they provide no motivation for adhering to them. To avoid legalistic minimalism, a focus on the kingdom and on personal vocation is absolutely essential, especially for Christians who lack mature virtues.

For all Christians, the true alternative to legalism lies in recognizing that everyone has a unique contribution to make in helping Jesus continue his redemptive work. As for virtues, Jesus is their source — "our wisdom, our righteousness and sanctification and redemption" (1 Cor 1:30). He not only models the virtues but communicates them to his disciples, provided they respond to his "Follow me" and cooperate wholeheartedly with him as he continues his saving work.

A Rich Young Man

The gospel story of the rich young man (or magistrate), told by Matthew, Mark, and Luke, helps make all this clearer. Here is Matthew's version:

> And behold, one came up to him, saying, "Teacher, what good deed must I do, to have eternal life?" And he said to him, "Why do you ask me about what is good? One there is who is good. If you would enter life, keep the commandments." He said to him, "Which?" And Jesus said, "You shall not kill, You shall not commit adultery, You shall not steal, You shall not bear false witness, Honor your father and mother, and, You shall love your neighbor as yourself." The young man said to him, "All these I have observed; what do I still lack?" Jesus said to him, "If you would be perfect, go, sell what you possess and give to the poor, and you will have treasure in heaven; and come, follow me." When the young man heard this he went away sorrowful; for he had great possessions. (Mt 19:16–22)

In Mark and Luke, too, Jesus promises his questioner "treasure in heaven" if he sells his possessions and follows Jesus (see Mk 17:21, Lk 18:22). Now, this treasure evidently must be something over and above eternal life, since eternal life is promised just for keeping the commandments. Is this "something over and above" intended only for an elite group, a hand-picked few? So it might seem — at first. Yet the passage as a whole can rightly be taken as addressed to everyone, since Jesus makes it clear elsewhere that everyone is invited to follow him.

How are we to untangle these seemingly tangled threads? As follows.

The young man needs to divest himself of his wealth in order to become a disciple. Not everyone needs to do that, though the poor are better off when it comes to following Jesus. But everyone *does* need to detach himself or herself from everyone and everything else in order to make a total commitment of self to Jesus and his kingdom. This is done by committing oneself not just to keeping the commandments but to doing *whatever* God wants, which involves trying to learn what that is and then doing it to the best of one's ability. In other words: discerning, accepting, and fulfilling a personal vocation.

This isn't something we do by ourselves. It is done by the Spirit of the Lord acting in us: "It is you who have accomplished all we have done" (Is 26:12 NAB). All is grace: the ability to act, the interest in acting, the free choice, the carrying out of the choice, the merit and the reward that come with doing so. All are God's gifts, which we need only accept. And part of that comprehensive grace is a life of good works, prepared in advance, as the Letter to the Ephesians says, for us to "walk in."

Even so, it is possible to give up many things without doing it for the sake of Jesus and the kingdom, without dedication to him and his cause. We see this happening all the time in the case of people busy pursuing their own agendas rather than God's: priests and religious who, finding themselves in assignments they don't like, tell their bishops or superiors, "This job is driving me crazy, and if you don't transfer me, I'm going to quit"; married men or women who say to their spouses of many years, "I'm sorry to have to tell you this, but there's someone else. And we're really in love!"

Faced with such confusion, one recalls something St. Ignatius of Loyola says in a section of his *Spiritual Exercises* (n. 169). We quoted it earlier: To choose rightly it is necessary to concentrate on "the end for which I am created, that is, for the praise of God and for the salvation of my soul."

But, Ignatius points out, some people make the mistake of confusing ends and means, and giving priority to the latter: "As a result, what they ought to seek first, they seek last." There are equivalents of the rich young man all around us. In fact, we ourselves may act as he did more often than we care to admit.

It is a serious mistake to suppose that the gospel and the world are compatible, or that some sort of comfortable compromise is possible between the two, so that Jesus' followers can live easily in the world. This error is the source of what Jacques Maritain called "kneeling to the world." Revealed truth (the "gospel") really is in radical, irreconcilable conflict with the corrupt secular culture (the "world"). The problem isn't with the world as God created it, but with the world as it now is, bent and mutilated by sin. Vatican II tells us that "a monumental struggle against the powers of darkness pervades the whole history of man. The battle was joined from the very origins of the world and will continue until the last day, as the Lord has attested" (Pastoral Constitution on the Church in the Modern World, *Gaudium et Spes,* n. 37).

Yet most followers of Christ are called to live their lives in the midst of this highly problematical world. In John's account of the Last Supper, Jesus speaks to the Father on his disciples' behalf: "I do not pray that thou shouldst take them out of the world, but that thou shouldst keep them from the evil one. . . . As thou didst send me into the world, so I have sent them into the world" (Jn 17:15, 18).

But sent us to do what? The answer is: To do our part in Jesus' ongoing redemptive work. Personal vocation is not a formula for worldly success. Jesus' followers can look forward to persecution and suffering, for that is how evil is bested and redemption comes about. Referring to the sinful world, Vatican II, just a few sentences after the one quoted above, teaches us that "if anyone wants to know how this unhappy situation can be overcome, Christians will tell him that all human activity, constantly imperiled by man's pride and deranged self-love, must be purified and perfected by the power of Christ's cross and resurrection." Christ's followers help bring that about in a multitude of different ways by the faithful living-out of their personal vocations.

Personal Vocation and Conversion

Where does conversion fit in? Let's look at one of the most famous conversions ever. If the story of St. Paul's conversion is the best-known conversion story of all time, St. Augustine's account of his own conversion is a close second. He tells the story in book eight of his *Confessions.*

Augustine was in his early thirties. Despite being a brilliant, rising rhetorician and philosopher, he had grown weary of his former way of life, filled with sins of lust and dalliance with contemporary intellectual fads. He felt himself increasingly drawn not just to God but to the Christian faith. "I was unhappy at the life I led in the world," he writes, "and it was indeed a heavy burden, for the hope of honor and profit no longer inflamed my desire as formerly to help me bear so exacting a servitude." But something held him back: "What still held me tight bound was my need of woman." Pulled this way and that, he says, "I came to understand what I had read, how the *flesh lusts against the spirit and the spirit against the flesh.*"

This continued for some time. "What is wrong with us?" Augustine demanded one day of his friend Alypius. "The unlearned arise and take heaven by force, and here are we with all our learning, stuck fast in flesh and blood!" Retiring into the garden of the house where he was staying in Milan, he wrestled furiously with himself. "Those trifles of all trifles, and vanities of vanities, my one-time mistresses, held me back, plucking at my garment of flesh, and murmuring softly: 'Are you sending us away?' And 'From this moment shall we not be with you, now or forever?' And 'From this moment shall this or that not be allowed you, now or forever?' " Questions familiar to many besides Augustine. Then:

> Such things I said, weeping in the most bitter sorrow of my heart. And suddenly I heard a voice from some nearby house, a boy's voice or a girl's voice, I do not know: but it was a sort of sing-song, repeated again and again, "Take and read, take and read." . . . Damming back the flood of my tears I arose, interpreting the incident as quite certainly a divine command to open my book of Scripture and read the passage at which I should open. . . . So I

was moved to return to the place where Alypius was sitting, for I had put down the Apostle's [Paul's] book there when I arose. I snatched it up, opened it and in silence read the passage upon which my eyes first fell: *Not in rioting and drunkenness, not in chambering and impurities, not in contention and envy, but put ye on the Lord Jesus Christ and make not provision for the flesh in its concupiscences* (Rom 13:13).

From that moment Augustine was a changed man.

Conversion is not the same as discerning a vocation, but the two things can hardly be separated. The conversion of heart that turns someone away from world and self, and toward others and God, is a necessary prior condition for discernment. The link is visible in the account of her conversion given by British spiritual writer Caryll Houselander in her memoirs, *A Rocking-Horse Catholic.*

Houselander died in 1954 at the age of fifty-three. At the time of the incident she relates, apparently in the mid-1920s, she was living in London, a spiritual and mental "displaced person," alienated from family, friends, and Church. Yet even in her loneliness, she writes (in a passage that recalls Dorothy Day), "I knew instinctively that mine was a curious kind of loneliness which could never be ended even by the closest relationship with individuals, but only, in some mysterious way which I could not yet understand, by some kind of communion with all men, everywhere in the world." One day, she recalls,

> I was in an underground train, a crowded train in which all sorts of people jostled together, sitting and strap-hanging — workers of every description going home at the end of the day. Quite suddenly I saw with my mind, but as vividly as a wonderful picture, Christ in them all. But I saw more than that; not only was Christ in every one of them, living in them, dying in them, rejoicing in them, sorrowing in them — but because He was in them, and because they were here, the whole world was here too, here in this underground train; not only the world as it was at that moment,

not only all the people in all the countries of the world, but all those people who had lived in the past, and all those yet to come.

The vision of "Christ in man" lingered for several days as its implications gradually became clear. For example: "the reverence that everyone must have for a sinner; instead of condoning his sin, which is in reality his utmost sorrow, one must comfort Christ who is suffering in him."

In sum, Houselander writes, this vision of Christ in human persons "altered the course of my life completely." It suffuses her writing with awareness that "the ordinary life itself [is] sacramental, and every action of anyone at all has an eternal meaning."

> Christ is everywhere; in Him every kind of life has a meaning and has an influence on every other kind of life. It is not the foolish sinner like myself, running about the world with reprobates and feeling magnanimous, who comes closest to them and brings them healing; it is the contemplative in her cell who has never set eyes on them, but in whom Christ fasts and prays for them — or it may be a charwoman in whom Christ makes Himself a servant again, or a king whose crown of gold hides a crown of thorns. Realization of our oneness in Christ is the only cure for human loneliness. For me, too, it is the only ultimate meaning of life, the only thing that gives meaning and purpose to every life.

Not everyone has dramatic, life-changing conversion experiences like those of St. Augustine and Caryll Houselander (although more people may have experiences more or less like them than is recognized in our skeptical, secularized day and age); but everyone is called by God to a continuing experience of conversion in his or her own particular way. For many, this is indispensable to seeing and accepting their personal vocations — and to the ongoing struggle to live them out in the face of failures and setbacks.

Pope John Paul II says as much in his apostolic exhortation on reconciliation and penance. Reflecting on the parable of the Prodigal Son, he writes:

This prodigal son is man — every human being: bewitched by the temptation to separate himself from his father in order to lead his own independent existence; disappointed by the emptiness of the mirage which had fascinated him; alone, dishonored, exploited when he tries to build a world all for himself; sorely tried, even in the depths of his own misery, by the desire to return to communion with his father. (*Reconciliatio et Paenitentia*, n. 5)

And, he says, like the father in the parable, "God looks out for the return of his child, embraces him when he arrives and orders the banquet of the new meeting with which the reconciliation is celebrated."

"Missing" One's Vocation

As the Holy Father suggests, repentant sinners have complete personal vocations. This is so even for those who sinfully make binding commitments they shouldn't have made or else fail, in ways that can't be corrected, to make the commitments they ought. But the question of missing one's vocation requires closer examination.

People who eventually come to a clear understanding of the idea of personal vocation and of their own personal vocations after having been ignorant of the question for a time often discover that, even though they hadn't been paying attention to God's plan for their lives, he managed to guide them — sometimes even by their own superficial desires and tastes — to do many things that prepared them for their callings. Likely now to have some things to repent, they will regret not having sooner understood how to shape their lives properly; but they still will find that God continues to offer them a plan for their lives that is the same in most respects as the one they previously ignored.

The situation is different, however, for those who, ignorant of vocation and wrongly motivated, profoundly shaped their lives in ways not for the best — for example, men called to be teaching brothers who became priests instead; women who should have remained single but instead married; people who turned their backs on worthwhile careers they should have pursued, for the sake of careers that promised more money and prestige.

Suppose such a person now sees the mistake. What should he or she do? Does that person still have a vocation?

As to what should be done: Having made commitments that others now depend on them to fulfill, people in this situation should certainly fulfill those commitments insofar as that can be done without doing something immoral. Thus, a couple who made a mistake in marrying each other and now have five children should stay married and raise their children; someone who divorced his or her spouse and entered a civil marriage must stop committing adultery with the second partner, yet he or she still has serious moral obligations to the second partner and to their children.

But do people like this still have vocations? If they repent and set about doing God's will, they will find that God does indeed have a complete plan for them, so that they still can make the most of the *rest* of their lives. In that sense, they have vocations, though not the ones they earlier spurned. God knows how to make good use even of the wrongdoing of sinners who repent and seek to become saints. He makes all things — all without exception — work together for the good of those who love him (see Rom 8:28). Think of Saul, who persecuted the Church. In later life, as Paul, he thought himself the least of the apostles (see 1 Cor 15:9), yet by God's grace he may have done more than any other to spread the faith and build up the Church.

True, some people do fail to accept their vocations. A woman wearing feminist blinders turns her back on her calling to be a wife and mother in order to have a career as a corporate lawyer; a man lets laziness and sensuality keep him from entering a demanding form of consecrated life or lay apostolate as God intends him to do. God still calls such people according to the circumstances of their lives. If they recognize their errors and repent, they can be sure God is calling them to the life of witness and service, the participation in the Church's mission, now available to them in their lives as they are.

Henry James tells an odd, parable-like tale about the missing of vocation in a story called *The Beast in the Jungle.* It is worth considering here because it gets the reality of vocation so painfully wrong.

The frequently anthologized story concerns a man named John Marcher who from his early years has a sense of being "kept for something rare and strange, possibly prodigious and terrible" — a destiny so out of the ordinary and (whatever it is) so threatening in its prodigious way that he must face it alone, without involving anyone else in his fate. Proceeding on this belief, he rejects the possibility of marriage with a charming woman who loves him.

After many years, she dies. Marcher visits her grave. While there, he observes a man at another grave consumed with grief for a loved one. "What had the man *had,*" Marcher wonders, "to make him by the loss of it so bleed and yet live?" Then he sees the truth. Here is the Beast in the Jungle: "The fate he had been marked for he had met with a vengeance — he had emptied the cup to the lees; he had been the man of his time, *the* man, to whom nothing on earth was to have happened."

This strange narrative may be read simply as the depiction of a psychological aberration. (It may be autobiographical to some extent; for even though Henry James certainly had friends, he was well known for avoiding emotional entanglements and never married.) Still, quite a few people, without going as far as John Marcher, find it difficult or impossible to settle down to a plan of life, to make commitments and stick to them; and they may imagine that they are waiting for their callings (their own special "beasts") to announce themselves.

God does not treat us like this, hiding our vocations from us despite our best efforts to learn what they are. God wants us to find, accept, and live our callings, and to that end he gives us all the helps we need. Instead of seeking applications to ourselves in Henry James's story, we should take our guidance from the parable of the vineyard laborers waiting for work (see Mt 20:1–16). The owner of the vineyard hires some of these men "early in the morning," more of them at the third, sixth, and ninth hours. Then, at the eleventh hour, "he went out and found others standing; and he said to them, 'Why do you stand here idle all day?' They said to him, 'Because no one has hired us.' He said to them, 'You go into the vineyard too' " (Mt 20:1, 6–7).

Early and late, God has work for us to do. If we do not hear his call, we are not listening.

When Burnout Strikes

Another problem of a vocational kind is what these days is called burn-out. Common among professionals who, having done the same work for a number of years, discover they've lost their taste for it, burnout typically manifests itself in loss of zest, restlessness, and a decline in professional performance. The unhesitating advice of a writer like Gail Sheehy would be: Quit and try something else you expect will be more personally rewarding.

Often, that would be a mistake. It's not that people should never change jobs and occupations — sometimes they should. Sometimes, in fact, radical changes are central to the experience of conversion, as in the case of a St. Paul or a St. Ignatius of Loyola (who gave up the life of a professional soldier to become an ardent apostle and founder of a new form of priestly life and service). Whether to change or not is a question of personal vocation to be settled by discernment. Burnout may be a sign that change is necessary; it is certainly among the data to take into consideration when discerning.

From a vocational point of view, nevertheless, people suffering burn-out shouldn't be in a rush to conclude the time has come to switch to something radically different. In entering their present field (retail sales, the military, teaching, whatever it may be), they made, or at least they *should* have made, a commitment to serve others. Now, experiencing distaste for their work, they should re-commit themselves to service. Or else make a commitment to it, if that wasn't done in the first place and they chose their particular line of work for the pay or the glamour or personal satisfaction.

If what they presently do doesn't allow them to serve others in ways that count (a doctor whose practice consists largely of unnecessary plastic surgery done to gratify the vanity of self-indulgent patients, a lawyer who spends her days finding loopholes for the wealthy to avoid taxes), they may be well advised to refocus on work in the same profession that offers opportunities for serving people in their real needs. But that is very different from quitting the profession entirely in favor of another field that — once again — seems to offer personal satisfaction, or else taking early retirement and killing time on expensive sightseeing trips or frivolous hobbies while dodging the question of vocation instead of facing it.

Vocational Formation and Catechesis

Vocational formation is a lifelong need for everyone, precisely because we all have to discern our personal vocations in the constantly changing circumstances of our lives. Still, vocational formation — the reality of personal vocation, the need to discern and how to do that, the steps to take in accepting and living out one's calling — is especially necessary for the young. Thus, Pope John Paul II says that "the fundamental and continuous attitude of the disciple should be one of vigilance and a conscious attentiveness to the voice of God" (On the Vocation and the Mission of the Lay Faithful in the Church and in the World, *Christifideles Laici,* n. 58).

The point of vocational formation is to foster this vigilance and conscientious attentiveness. But how?

Raising the question of personal vocation should begin in the religious education of children soon after first confession and first Communion. Pastors should see to it that it does. Addressing the question of vocation is a responsibility of parents, of course, and it should be done in the home. But not only there, for it also should be part of the formal catechetical instruction of children in Catholic schools and religious education programs.

The central points of this instruction should be obvious by now. God has given us everything. Jesus laid down his life for us. What should we give back to God to show our gratitude and love? We become one with Jesus in the Eucharist and, in him, enter into communion with one another. How can we cooperate with him in this work? What is our role in the mission of the Church, which carries on Christ's mission here and now?

Since young children seldom are in a position to discern future elements of their personal vocations, they should not be pressured to make premature commitments. Telling a small boy, "How happy your family and the pastor and your teachers and everybody else will be if you grow up to be a great athlete!" or a little girl, "It would make your mother and father very proud if you became an executive!" may do more to arouse self-centered desires or instill feelings of resentment and guilt than to encourage a true calling to athletic excellence or service in the business world.

On the other hand, small children *do* have vocations here and now — to do their best at the things they must do and to be *good* small children — cooperative with their parents and teachers, respectful to other adults, kind to siblings and schoolmates, careful not to break things or make messes, quick to say "please" and "thank you," and so on. Without using the technical language of vocation, the adults who are responsible for children's formation should tell them clearly that these things are what God asks of them at this point in their lives.

Before adolescence, too, children can and should be encouraged to begin asking themselves what Jesus would have them do in the more important matters that are left up to them — the friends to make, the school activities to become involved in, and so on. They also should be encouraged to begin praying about their personal vocation, in the knowledge that, beyond the small things he asks of them now, God soon will be calling them to larger, more life-shaping deeds and commitments. Unless ideas and practices relevant to the vocational question take root before the teenage years, when children reach that tumultuous period they will organize their lives in ways having little or nothing to do with personal vocation and, very likely, in conflict with faith. Living out that sort of agenda then will lead them to commit many venial sins and will generate temptations to commit mortal sins and perhaps even to abandon the faith.

Unhappy parents often ask why their children don't go to church, are living outside wedlock with their girlfriends or boyfriends, and in other ways seem spiritually and morally adrift. Every case is different, but often the same factors are at work. The pattern described here — consistent neglect of the question of personal vocation until, humanly speaking, it's too late for the parents to do any good by raising it — very often is among them.

Assuming the sacrament of confirmation is administered between the ages of twelve and fourteen, catechesis for children from first Communion until then should prepare for confirmation, with increasing attention devoted to the themes of personal vocation and apostolate. This is not imposing something extrinsic on the sacrament but recognizing its essential nature as a sacrament of apostolate.

About those who receive confirmation, Vatican Council II makes the point that "the Holy Spirit endows them with special strength so that they are more strictly obliged to spread and defend the faith, both by word and by deed, as true witnesses of Christ" (Dogmatic Constitution on the Church, *Lumen Gentium,* n. 11). In confirmation, a person who became God's child in baptism receives a specific mandate, and is given specific strength, to take up the family business of sharing God's truth and life.

The Meaning of Apostolate

But if confirmation is a sacrament of apostolate, what does apostolate mean? Unfortunately, the word is seldom heard today.

Before the Second Vatican Council, Catholics commonly supposed that only specifically religious activities qualified as apostolate. The apostolate therefore was thought to be mainly and properly the work of bishops and priests and, by extension, religious. Although lay apostolate was recognized and often commended, it was seen as something lay people might do as a way of helping and collaborating with priests. Catholic Action, the preeminent model of lay apostolate before Vatican II, was officially defined as the participation of lay people in the apostolate of the hierarchy.

Vatican II took a greatly expanded view. Explaining that the Church was founded "for the purpose of spreading the kingdom of Christ throughout the earth for the glory of God the Father, to enable all men to share in His saving redemption, and that through them the whole world might enter into a relationship with Christ," the Council taught:

> All activity of the Mystical Body directed to the attainment of this goal is called the apostolate, which the Church carries on in various ways through all her members. For the Christian vocation by its very nature is also a vocation to the apostolate. (Decree on the Apostolate of Lay People, *Apostolicam Actuositatem,* n. 2)

This is true of bishops, priests, deacons, and religious. And the laity? They, too, are called to share in evangelization; but they also are called to exercise their apostolate in *all* daily activities belonging to the temporal order:

> But the laity likewise share in the priestly, prophetic, and royal office of Christ and therefore have their own share in the mission of the whole people of God in the Church and in the world. They exercise the apostolate in fact by their activity directed to the evangelization and sanctification of men and to the penetrating and perfecting of the temporal order through the spirit of the Gospel. In this way, their temporal activity openly bears witness to Christ and promotes the salvation of men. Since the laity, in accordance with their state of life, live in the midst of the world and its concerns, they are called by God to exercise their apostolate in the world like leaven, with the ardor of the spirit of Christ. (Ibid.)

Lest there be any doubt about the source of the laity's mission, the Council immediately adds, "Incorporated into Christ's Mystical Body through Baptism and strengthened by the power of the Holy Spirit through Confirmation, they are assigned to the apostolate by the Lord Himself" (ibid, n. 3).

Vatican II transformed the old dichotomy between temporal things and spiritual things, which for a long time had been a serious obstacle to clear thinking about lay spirituality, lay apostolate, and the vocations of lay people. True, temporal things and spiritual things *are* different and shouldn't be confused with one another or treated as interchangeable. But the Council emphatically rejects the idea that spiritual and temporal exist in separate, watertight compartments, that the spiritual is always superior and the temporal always inferior, and that the involvement of lay people in secular affairs inescapably condemns them to second-class status in regard to the things that really count.

First of all, the Council says, temporal affairs have a natural goodness of their own.

> All those things which make up the temporal order, namely, the good things of life and the prosperity of the family, culture, economic matters, the arts and professions, the laws of the political community, international relations, and other matters of this kind, as well as their development and progress, not only aid in the attainment of man's ultimate goal but also possess their own intrinsic value. This value has been established in them by God, whether they are considered in themselves or as parts of the whole temporal order. "God saw that all He had made was very good" (Gen. 1:31). (*Apostolicam Actuositatem*, n. 7)

To be sure, sin is a reality in human history and human life, and "the use of temporal things has been marred by serious vices." But this only underlines the duty of Christians and especially of the laity. Although the "whole Church must work vigorously in order that men may become capable of rectifying the distortion of the temporal order and directing it to God through Christ," nevertheless lay people "must take up the renewal of the temporal order as their own special obligation" (ibid.).

Moreover, the Council makes clear, the effort that is called for extends even into the realm of the spiritual, since, as we saw in the last chapter, the "renewal of the temporal order" involves nothing less than preparing material for God's kingdom. There, as the Pastoral Constitution on the Church in the Modern World explains, we shall find once more "all the good fruits of our nature and effort . . . but cleansed of all dirt, lit up, and transformed" (*Gaudium et Spes,* n. 39). It is essential to keep all this clearly in mind when considering apostolate and personal vocation in general and the apostolates and personal vocations of lay people in particular; for this vision lies at the heart of what it means for them to embrace their vocations and participate in the mission of the Church.

A Full-time, Lifelong Task

Personal vocation is, as it were, a lens that brings the details of one's life of faith into focus. As such, it is the medium by which confirmation organizes the life of someone who is confirmed. Clearly, though, there isn't a lot for the sacrament to organize and strengthen in the case of people who fail to recognize and embrace their vocations. The life of faith remains at best disorganized and unfocused for them.

As we saw above, there are no free areas in the life of someone trying to live out a personal vocation. Everything should find a place within it and be related to apostolic responsibilities. Does this mean Christians must be religious fanatics, single-mindedly fixated on religion and ignoring everything else? Certainly not.

All human goods can have a place in the life of someone who seeks to participate in them in morally upright ways. That includes truth and knowledge, friendship, physical vitality and health, recreation and aesthetic satisfaction, and all the rest — along with, but hardly limited to, religion. Furthermore, almost every individual's personal vocation necessarily will involve multiple commitments, harmonious and integrated with one another, that carry with them a variety of roles — spouse, parent, child, friend, worker, neighbor, parishioner, many others besides. There is nothing narrow or fanatical about a life like this, and anyone who really *was* a religious fanatic would have gotten Christian life and vocation terribly wrong.

Yet many people, including decent, church-going people, seldom or never think about their vocations because it has never been suggested to them that they should. That plainly is true today of many young people. Personal vocation had no place in their religious formation; the only "vocations" talk was an occasional reference to priesthood and consecrated life as desirable callings. Now, setting sail on the stormy seas of adolescence, with all its emotional turmoil and sexual temptations, they are unlikely to think spontaneously about their vocations, unlikely to become aware that God has a special plan in mind for them — a plan they need to discern and accept.

In these circumstances it's hardly surprising that so many young Catholics give little or no serious thought to the priesthood and consecrated life, and look on marriage and career as pathways to personal gratification. The solution is to make catechesis about personal vocation and apostolate — beginning after First Communion and continuing from then on — a central part of the formation provided in Catholic schools and religious education programs, and by any other pastoral care of children and adolescents. Unless that happens, there is little realistic chance that young people will make their life decisions, whatever they are, as Christian commitments.

Vocational formation must continue throughout life, for discerning one's personal vocation amid changing circumstances is an ongoing task. Pope John Paul II lists the elements of this process as spiritual formation, doctrinal formation, and "the cultivation of human values" (*Christifideles Laici,* n. 60).

Spiritual formation: Lay people shouldn't compartmentalize their lives, separating spiritual interests from everyday occupations and activities. Instead, they need to integrate the two. The aim, John Paul says, is their growth in the spiritual life "through the very performance of their tasks according to God's will."

Doctrinal formation: Lay Catholics need to understand the faith well in order to present it credibly to others. The need is particularly evident today, when so many otherwise well-educated Catholics are woefully ignorant of their own religious tradition. In particular, those who have public responsibilities require a thorough grounding in Catholic social doctrine to play a responsible part in politics and public life.

Formation in human values: Explaining the kind of formation he has in mind under this heading, John Paul repeats teaching of Vatican II, that the lay faithful "should also hold in high esteem professional skill, family and civic spirit, and the virtues related to social behavior, namely, honesty, a spirit of justice, sincerity, courtesy, moral courage; without them there is no true Christian life."

All this amounts to a daunting challenge. But who can doubt that formation like this is needed?

To Various Groups

Nearing the end of this book, we want to address a few words to certain groups with special responsibilities for forming others about vocation. Of course, everything already said also applies to these groups, as it does to everyone. But there are some particular points that parents, teachers, and bishops and pastors especially need to keep in mind.

To parents

All good parents want their children to be happy, and being happy is commonly thought to mean being successful, as success is understood by people of the parents' background and social class. Problems can arise here.

The journalist David Brooks suggests that a typical suburban American male today (with only a few adjustments, this fits women, too) entertains an ideal of success more or less along these lines: "Your DVD library is organized, and so is your walk-in closet. Your car is clean and vacuumed, your frequently dialed numbers are programmed into your cell phone, your telephone plan is suited to your needs, and your various gizmos interface without conflict. Your wife is effortlessly slender, your kids are unnaturally bright, your job is rewarding, your promotions are inevitable, and you look great in casual slacks."

We smile at this. But why? Not because it is a far-out fantasy but because it cuts too close for comfort. Perhaps no one's idea of the Good Life is quite *that* shallow, but a lot of us want something not so awfully different, for ourselves and our kids.

The trouble with this idea of success is that it falls tragically short of what a truly good life can and should be. The reader won't be surprised when we say that, from a Christian point of view, real happiness — the

Good Life that God intends for us — lies in discerning, accepting, and faithfully living out our personal vocations.

The most important thing parents can do in relation to the personal vocations of their children is give good example. If, up to this time, parents who've begun to catch on to the idea of personal vocation have not shaped their own lives entirely by that principle, they need to begin. This is likely to include reconsidering, and perhaps adjusting or even giving up, elements of their lives and lifestyle previously thought to be without moral significance. And rather than keeping what they are giving up and why a secret from their children, they should be quite open with any of them who are old enough to understand.

All parents will need to look for God's will in new challenges and opportunities as they arise — things like whether to take a new job or buy a bigger house, and how to deal with serious illnesses and setbacks. Seldom will it be necessary to conceal things from the kids. If it is not necessary, then the process of discernment should be conducted in such a way that they are exposed to it and even contribute to the extent they can. Buy a bigger house? Encourage the children to enter into the discussion by pointing out pros and cons. Among other things, they will learn a lot from observing what mom and dad treat as relevant to discerning and which of their emotions they act on.

Parents also need to give their children example by their fidelity in fulfilling commitments, among which the commitment to be conscientious, loving parents is hardly the least. Parents teach their children to serve others unselfishly and find personal fulfillment in it precisely by finding their own fulfillment in parenting and in subordinating to it other self-interests — hobbies, recreation, socializing with friends, getting and enjoying material possessions, and so on.

Since each person must discern his or her own personal vocation, parents should not develop an agenda of their own for their children and then try to sell it to them, much less force it upon them. Of course there are some things kids must do, and parents should encourage them to do what they must, and to do it well and gladly. But where there are legitimate options, kids should be allowed to shape their own lives.

Suppose fifth-grader Eddie has a variety of sports and other activities available to him at his school. Eddie's folks shouldn't press him to do this or that, but should encourage him to discern what he will do. At the same time, they should call his attention to possibilities he might overlook, point out reasons for and against doing this or that, and otherwise be helpful. But finally the judgment should be his. Eddie and all other children mature better and make firmer commitments in the long run by learning to discern and respond to their own vocations at as early an age as possible.

And success? Something Mother Teresa of Calcutta said about that is frequently quoted: God does not expect us to be successful but to be faithful.

This is a very consoling thought when, having tried to do what we thought was right, the result is failure, even disaster, for ourselves and perhaps others, too. But the saying has another, more important meaning: We should *never* be concerned about success and should always be concerned *only* with being faithful.

Instead of organizing our lives by developing and pursuing agendas — goals and objectives we think embody happiness — we should shape our lives according to our personal vocations and make our own the goals and objectives we believe God wants us to seek. But even where these goals and objectives are concerned, we shouldn't become overly attached, and should be open to discovering that although God wanted us to try, he didn't mean for us to succeed, or else meant us to succeed only partly, while facing challenges we never expected along the way. This is what parents need to teach their children about success.

The key question is what one means by success. In an obvious sense, people succeed when the actions they choose produce the benefits they have in view. But no action by itself ever is sufficient to accomplish that, for other things also must go right. For instance, it isn't enough for a farmer to plant seeds and put down fertilizer to guarantee a bountiful harvest. Drought and insects still can ruin the crop. Success is never certain, and even when achieved it may bring unforeseen, bad side effects. We never know enough or have enough control over events for our actions to bring about the ideal situation that at heart we want — a world in which everyone is richly fulfilled by every benefit, with no bad side effects at all.

Yet we *can* have confident hope of such a world. It is the kingdom God revealed through Christ. It began with his resurrection from the dead. Mary became fully part of it at her Assumption; and everyone who dies and rises in Christ will be added to it. This is the kingdom Vatican II speaks of in *Gaudium et Spes,* n. 39 — the new earth and new heaven where those who serve the Lord will find the fulfillment of their every good hope.

Really, it makes no sense to focus on success in this life. What matters is that in each situation we do our best to see God's will for us, commit ourselves to it, and carry it out faithfully. The rest can and should be left to God. Sometimes we will succeed as the world understands success, other times not. But in the long run we will always succeed by shaping our lives this way, whereas in pursuing our own agendas we can be sure of failing even when we do "succeed."

Parents make an enormously important contribution to the vocational formation of their children by teaching them these things.

To teachers

Since Vatican Council II, the pendulum in catechesis has swung sharply away from legalism and from an excessive emphasis on sin and punishment, good works and merit. Although this is a welcome development in itself, the pendulum has swung too far, resulting in a de-emphasizing of moral responsibility that mirrors the permissiveness of today's secular culture.

Without lapsing into legalism or the kind of neo-Pelagianism that suggests grace and salvation are *earned* by our good deeds, the education of children and young people needs to include a balanced emphasis on personal responsibility and service. This should take in more than just their current responsibilities and the "service projects" now popular in schools and educational programs. Although service projects often may be good in themselves, they are not good to the extent they lend support to the notion that serving others is a part-time, now-and-then kind of responsibility for Christians. Instead of channeling kids into short-term service projects during proximate preparation for confirmation or over spring break, schools should help them start discerning and living out their personal vocations — of which service to others not only now but in the future is certainly a key part.

If what we have said throughout this book about personal vocation is correct, it would be a mistake for teachers, when speaking about vocations, to speak only of the priesthood and consecrated life.

Those two possibilities can and should be presented as desirable options that unquestionably are elements in the personal vocations of some. But the impression shouldn't be given either that they are the *only* callings or that any state of life is by itself anyone's complete vocation. It also would be wrong to imply, as even these days still seems to happen, that, while one can be called to marry, the priesthood and consecrated life are the genuinely *big* callings, the truly *serious* vocations that really count.

Still, teachers should certainly speak to their students about vocation. It would be an inexcusable omission to fail to do that in the presumably friendly setting of a Catholic school or religious education program. If such a school or program understands its job as being simply to prepare students to earn a living, fulfill community responsibilities that even non-believers recognize, and/or meet the minimal requirements of Catholic practice, it falls hopelessly short of the mark.

The essential point to communicate is the idea of personal vocation, along with practical advice on discerning. So much the better if the school or educational program provides opportunities for reflection, prayer, and discernment — retreats, days of recollection, and the like.

It can be hard work today explaining personal vocation to children and young people, who, like their parents, have been victimized by a steady stream of propaganda and indoctrination on behalf of secular notions of success along with the pop-psychology of "passages." So, along with raising the question of vocation, it will be necessary to confront the obstacles and objections that probably already exist in students' minds.

The document of the European vocations congress cited earlier speaks of the need to "help young people uncover the basic misunderstanding: the all too worldly and me-centered interpretation of life."

The young person needs to be stimulated by lofty ideals, considering something which goes beyond him and is beyond his capacities, because of which it is worthwhile giving one's life. . . . To ask of a young person something that is less than his possibilities means offending his dignity and impeding his full self-realization; in a more positive way, the young person should be asked for the best he can give so that he may become and be himself.

Teachers must try to motivate those they teach, and it makes an enormous difference what sorts of motives they propose.

Motivating children by their pre-existing, subjective wants and goals reinforces those wants and goals. But children today very often are corrupted by appeals from the secular culture that encourage their ambitions for wealth, status, and pleasure. Instead, it is constructive to help children acknowledge their own gifts and limitations, and to call attention to opportunities for service and challenges that need to be met. It is very helpful to clarify and support their faith, not least by using saints as models, so that they will appreciate the priority of God's kingdom and the unimportance of worldly success. (Obviously, teachers in public schools have to proceed cautiously here.)

Students whose teachers are visibly living *their* vocations are more likely to pick up the idea than those whose teachers are ambitious careerists or are simply going through the motions of doing a job they don't much like. One of the most important things teachers can do for their students, Pope John Paul says, is to show by their lives what vocational commitment means. That holds true for Christian teachers at all levels — from nursery school through graduate and professional school. They should be "true witnesses of the gospel," he insists, "through their example of life, their professional competence and uprightness, their Christian inspired teaching" (*Christifideles Laici*, n. 62). Thus, teachers who can't offer their lives as worthy models to the children and young people they teach ought either to repent and reform or else find some other line of work.

John Paul also urges parents, teachers, clergy, religious, and young people themselves consciously to organize themselves as a "formation community" in the setting of the school. And — surprisingly perhaps but realistically — he makes the point that Catholic schools and educational programs should concentrate first of all on forming parents. "What is needed," he says, "is to prepare the lay faithful to dedicate themselves to the work of rearing their children as a true and proper part of Church mission" (ibid.). In other words: Help parents understand that their parenting itself is apostolic work that belongs to their vocation.

To bishops and others involved in vocation work

In the United States and many other countries, the bishops and some religious orders sponsor national vocations offices. Many dioceses have vocations offices of their own, as do some provinces of religious institutes. There are organizations, publications, and conferences devoted to vocations. All in all, it's an impressive picture in institutional and programmatic terms.

And, in almost all cases, these efforts are focused almost exclusively on vocations to the priesthood and consecrated life. The intentions are excellent, but it's a terrible mistake.

Our reservations don't concern the complaint sometimes heard these days that vocations personnel in some cases have encouraged unsuitable candidates for priesthood and consecrated life while discouraging or even refusing suitable ones. Where this really happened, it is inexcusable. But it isn't the point here. Rather, the point is the same one we have made repeatedly: For both theoretical and practical reasons, it is a serious error to treat vocation as a calling to the priesthood or consecrated life and only that.

Congratulations and thanks are in order to the bishops, religious superiors, vocation directors, pastors, and others who, troubled about the declining number of priests and religious in the United States and some other countries, have re-doubled efforts to identify and encourage new candidates. But as long as vocation is equated with the priestly or religious calling, these efforts seem certain to fall short of the need.

For a satisfactory number of new candidates for the priesthood and consecrated life to emerge, it will be essential to begin with, and scrupulously respect, the reality of personal vocation and what flows from it:

Not *recruitment* but *discernment* is the great need in vocations work today. Rather than focusing on increasing the numbers of seminarians and novices, bishops and religious superiors, diocesan vocation directors and the teams forming novices ought to focus on discerning God's plans with respect to those they might eventually ordain or approve for profession.

Moreover, discerning their personal vocations is a duty for all members of the Church. "If at one time vocations promotion referred only or mainly to certain vocations," says the European vocations congress quoted above, "now it must tend ever more toward the promotion of *all* vocations, because in the Lord's Church either we grow together or no one grows." As more people respond to the challenge, more will find they are called to be priests and religious, while many others will discern callings to other forms of committed participation in the Church's mission.

Taking this as the starting-point for vocation work, what should bishops and others do?

One thing that needs doing is to reorganize the vocation offices and revise their programs and literature to put personal vocation first. The message currently being communicated should be examined and in many cases probably amended. Serious-minded and properly motivated young people whom God is calling to priesthood and religious life are more likely to be repelled than attracted by the suggestion that such a calling is something like an invitation into an elite club. And those who might actually find such elitism attractive either aren't suitable candidates or else need help in clarifying and rectifying their motives.

Bishops need to write pastoral letters and preach about personal vocation. Confirmation homilies are particularly appropriate occasions for doing this. Pastors and other priests should consistently incorporate this theme into their preaching, too. Bishops also would do well, as the European congress points out, to bring pastoral work for vocations "out of its circle of experts" and "into the life of Christian parish communities." The experts and specialists have an important contribution to make, but so does everyone else.

That specifically is true of vocations to the priesthood and consecrated life. In the early Church the Christian community called people to service. Today, some priests and religious report that no one ever raised the question of vocation with them. Certainly a vocation of any kind is a calling from God, but human cooperation ordinarily is required for God's call to be heard. While no one should be subjected to pressure, Pope John Paul rightly cautions against hanging back; "a clear invitation, made at the right time, can be decisive in eliciting from young people a free and genuine response," he remarks in his document on the priesthood (I Will Give You Shepherds, *Pastores Dabo Vobis,* n. 39).

Annually, the bishop should urge everyone in the diocese to keep an eye out for persons they think would make good permanent deacons, priests, or religious; to speak to these people about looking into the possibility; and to pass on their names to a diocesan priest or a member of a religious community for which they seem suited. Bishops and religious superiors themselves need to be personally, immediately available to potential candidates, taking the initiative in getting in touch with individuals and saying, "I've heard about you, and I wonder if the Lord is calling you."

Since, as we saw above, the *Catechism of the Catholic Church* overlooks personal vocation, there is a real danger that catechisms based on it will do the same, despite the teaching of Vatican II and John Paul II making the importance of personal vocation clear. Bishops will need to make a special effort to get the idea included in catechetical programs. If they cannot immediately bring about its introduction into the catechetical textbook series they prefer, they should have special units on personal vocation prepared and used as supplementary material.

Bishops and pastors should see to it that teachers in Catholic schools and religious education programs understand personal vocation. They should take great care in hiring teachers, and certainly should *not* hire those who won't offer a good model for children. Bishops also should see to it that personal vocation gets its due in programs for training teachers and catechists.

And in marriage preparation programs as well. Many couples just want to get married as part of their personal agenda, and have given little or no thought to what God wants. Unfortunately, their motives may not include service — having and raising children for the kingdom, helping each other get there, witnessing to the mutual love of Christ and his Church. Given the way they have been trained and indoctrinated, some of these couples won't buy into the idea of personal vocation even if it is presented to them. But if it is presented properly, some will. In doing so, they will be taking an important step toward having happy, Christian marriages and toward properly catechizing their children when the time comes.

From time to time, bishops, priests, deacons, and religious also need to re-examine, renew, and if necessary rectify their own vocational commitments, not with the aim of changing them but to deepen and strengthen them. People sometimes enter the priesthood or consecrated life for inadequate and somehow self-centered reasons, and then stay due to inertia, convenience, or careerism — the expectation of a better parish, a bigger diocese, a more interesting assignment. Clergy and religious who find themselves in this situation need to repent and change. For the sake of God and the people they are meant to serve — and for their own sakes, too — they must become vibrant witnesses to authentic vocational commitment if they are to avoid disaster in their own lives and have much hope of interesting others in their way of life.

Finally, for pastoral reasons, bishops and others engaged in vocation work need to understand that vocational recruitment isn't a numbers game meant to fill slots so that ecclesiastical institutions can stay in business. At the heart of the question of personal vocation lies the question of holiness.

These callings are, to repeat, the lives of good works God means to be both people's paths to the heavenly kingdom and material for it. In a fundamental sense, of course, every Christian has a vocation to be a saint. This is the universal call to holiness of which Vatican Council II spoke (see *Lumen Gentium,* Chapter V). But it is personal vocation that provides the concrete, detailed plan for each individual's life of sanctity.

In treating the duty of bishops to sanctify, Vatican II says they "should be diligent in fostering holiness among their clerics, religious, and laity according to the special vocation of each" individual (Decree on the Pastoral Office of the Bishops in the Church, *Christus Dominus,* n. 15). This requires teaching about personal vocation — what it is, how to discern it, the importance of accepting it, the duty to be faithful to the commitments it entails — appropriate catechesis, at appropriate times, with personal vocation as its focus. As the Council remarks elsewhere, "Ceremonies however beautiful, or associations however flourishing, will be of little value if they are not directed toward the education of men to Christian maturity." To promote that, priests must help their people "to see what is required and what is God's will in the important and unimportant events of life" (Decree on the Ministry and Life of Priests, *Presbyterorum Ordinis,* n. 6).

In a May, 1993, audience talk, Pope John Paul made a very clear statement — insisting upon the teaching of Vatican Council II — about the duty of bishops and priests to help each of the faithful find, accept, and faithfully fulfill his or her personal vocation. "The community dimension of pastoral care . . . cannot overlook the needs of the individual faithful," he declared.

> As we read in the Council: "It is the priests' part as instructors in the faith to see to it either personally or through others that each member of the faithful shall be led in the Holy Spirit to the full development of his own vocation in accordance with the gospel teaching, to sincere and active charity and to the liberty with which Christ has set us free" (Decree on the Ministry and Life of Priests, *Presbyterorum Ordinis,* n. 6). The Council stresses the need to help each member of the faithful to discover his specific vocation, as a proper, characteristic task of the pastor who wants to respect and promote each one's personality. One could say that by his own example Jesus himself, the Good Shepherd who "calls his own sheep by name" (cf. Jn 10:3–4), has set the standard of individual pastoral care: knowledge and a relationship of friendship with individual persons. It is the presbyter's task to help each one to utilize well his own gift, and rightly to exercise the freedom that comes from Christ's salvation, as St. Paul urges (cf. Gal 4:3; 5:1, 13; cf. also Jn 8:36).

This is a call for personal spiritual direction about vocation for each Catholic willing to receive it.

While John Paul exhorts bishops and priests as much as possible to provide this direction themselves, they obviously cannot do it all, but will need to work "through others." One way of doing that is by training suitable lay people to give direction. In how many dioceses and parishes is anything like that now being done? The answer is embarrassingly obvious. Here is an appropriate, badly needed form of lay ministry, implicitly prescribed by Vatican II, that nevertheless has been virtually ignored up to this time.

Bishops also must see to it that their seminarians learn about personal vocation, so that in their future pastoral work they can preach and catechize about it, and give people sound, individual direction. For that to happen, personal vocation must be a central element in the moral theology program of seminaries. That means giving more time to this subject and less to some others (e.g., the time now often spent summarizing dissenting theological opinions and the disputes to which they have given rise or to laying out various theories about virtues). This shift in emphasis will help seminarians themselves to shake loose from the clericalist idea that their vocation is just to get ordained, and to realize that it embraces the whole of their lives, whether they ever get ordained or not.

The Electric Blanket and the Cross

God acts first. A personal vocation comes from him and is his plan for a person's unique cooperation with him. But God also gives all of us the grace to make free commitments to this calling and to live the lives of good deeds he intends. Here is a covenant of love and fidelity between a human person and God, fulfilled on the human side by the living out of a personal vocation and on God's side by the final perfecting of the individual with all the blessings of eternal life.

The distinguished American novelist and short story writer Flannery O'Connor is a striking instance of someone who over time came to see, accept, and live out a personal vocation ever more perfectly and purely. Earlier, we noted her pungent account of the destructive impact that clericalist thinking has on Catholics' understanding of vocation and apostolate. The central commitments of her own calling were to be a writer (and not just any kind of writer, but a deliberately, consciously Catholic one) and to carry the cross of illness and suffering.

She was born in Savannah, Georgia, on March 25, 1925, the feast of the Annunciation, the only child of Regina Cline and Edward Francis O'Connor, Jr., and was baptized Mary Flannery. Her parents were practicing Catholics of Irish-American descent, and their daughter attended parochial schools in her native city.

In 1926 Edward O'Connor, a realtor and builder, launched his own business, the Dixie Realty Company, but soon he began to have health problems. His condition was diagnosed as lupus, an incurable collagen disease in which the immune system attacks the body's own vital tissues. Enmeshed in growing financial difficulties associated with the depression of the 1930s and burdened by his illness, he took a job as an FHA real estate appraiser in 1938, and the family shifted to Atlanta. Shortly, Mary Flannery and her mother moved to the Cline family home in Milledgeville, Georgia, where the girl attended an experimental high school and drew cartoons and wrote for the school paper. Eventually Edward O'Connor joined his wife and daughter in Milledgeville. He died there of lupus February 1, 1941.

After graduating from high school, the young woman took an accelerated three-year wartime program at Georgia State College for Women. She majored in sociology and English, wrote stories and poems for the literary magazine, was art editor of the yearbook, and, says a biographer, took "an active part in student life, except for dances and sports." She also developed a close relationship with a young marine, but soon after the war he entered the seminary to become a priest.

Having enrolled in Iowa State University in 1945 with a scholarship to study journalism, O'Connor was admitted to the university's prestigious Writers' Workshop, and there was taught by experienced writers who encouraged her talent. Now she began signing her papers "Flannery." She also began attending daily Mass.

In 1948–49, having begun to sell stories and working on a novel, she spent half a year at a foundation-sponsored artists' colony near Saratoga

Springs, New York, where she became friends with some of the leading literary intellectuals of the day while attending Mass with the domestic staff. Next she lived for a year in New York City. Riding the train home to Milledgeville for the Christmas holidays in 1950, she became dangerously ill with a high fever. Lupus was diagnosed. At Emory University Hospital in Atlanta she received blood transfusions and massive doses of the cortisone derivative ACTH.

And there the story ends? As a matter of fact, the external events of Flannery O'Connor's life do very nearly come to a halt at this point, although she lived another thirteen years. The little there is to tell concerns the quiet routine of farm life (she enjoyed raising peacocks), hospital stays, occasional campus lecture tours to earn money, a pilgrimage to Rome and Lourdes (where she prayed, as she later reported, "for my book, not my bones"), and extensive correspondence. She fell in love with a man, but nothing came of it.

And, of course, there was the writing — a stream of stories and novels that won the apparently reclusive Georgia woman growing recognition as one of the most gifted literary artists of the day. Her first novel, *Wise Blood*, appeared in 1952, her second, *The Violent Bear It Away*, in 1960. Her short stories were collected as *A Good Man Is Hard to Find* (1955) and, posthumously, as *Everything That Rises Must Converge* (1965).

In February, 1964, O'Connor underwent surgery to remove a fibroid tumor that was causing anemia. ("If they don't make haste and get rid of it," she wrote a friend, "they will have to remove me and leave it.") Apparently the surgery reactivated the lupus. Her physical condition deteriorated rapidly. On July 7 she received the sacrament of the sick. Soon after, she learned that her short story *Revelation* had won first prize in an important literary competition. At the end of the month she was admitted to Baldwin County Hospital. On August 2 she slipped into a coma; a little after midnight August 3 she died of kidney failure. Her Requiem Mass was celebrated at Sacred Heart Church, Milledgeville, and she was buried in Memory Hill Cemetery beside her father.

If this record is comparatively skimpy, the record of her interior life is rich and full. It exists in her letters — humorous, vivacious, down-to-earth, often profound. Written to a large body of friends and admirers, they provide, along with much else, a running account of her understanding, acceptance, and living out of her vocation.

First of all, her vocation as a Catholic writer. "The ironical part of my silent reception by Catholics," she once wrote, "is the fact that I write the way I do because and only because I am a Catholic."

> I feel that if I were not a Catholic, I would have no reason to write, no reason to see, no reason ever to feel horrified or even to enjoy anything. I am a born Catholic, went to Catholic schools in my early years, and have never left or wanted to leave the Church. I have never had the sense that being a Catholic is a limit to the freedom of the writer, but just the reverse. Mrs. Tate [the writer Caroline Gordon] told me that after she became a Catholic, she felt she could use her eyes and accept what she saw for the first time, she didn't have to make a new universe for each book but could take the one she found. I feel myself that being a Catholic has saved me a couple of thousand years in learning to write.

Faith also supplied her fundamental theme: "It seems to me that all good stories are about conversion, about a character's changing."

> The action of grace changes a character. . . . Part of the difficulty of all this is that you write for an audience who doesn't know what grace is and don't recognize it when they see it. All my stories are about the action of grace on a character who is not very willing to support it, but most people think of these stories as hard, hopeless, brutal, etc.

It would be an exaggeration to call Flannery O'Connor's fiction Catholic apologetics, but she was undoubtedly aware of herself as a kind of cultural subversive engaged in infiltrating the secularized world of contemporary American letters with a message it didn't want to hear. "You probably have not imagined what it is to write as a Catholic, knowing that most of the people who read you will think what you believe is utter rubbish," she told a correspondent.

And in an article she explained that in religiously arid times like these, "writers who see by the light of their Christian faith" are bound to have "the sharpest eyes for the grotesque, for the perverse, and for the unacceptable."

> The novelist with Christian concerns will find in modern life distortions which are repugnant to him, and his problem will be to make these appear as distortions to an audience which is used to seeing them as natural; and he may well be forced to take ever more violent means to get his vision across to this hostile audience. When you can assume that your audience holds the same beliefs you do, you can relax a little and use more normal ways of talking to it; when you have to assume that it does not, then you have to make your vision apparent by shock — to the hard of hearing you shout, and for the almost blind you draw large and startling figures.

This is the Flannery O'Connor who on one occasion, having put up as long as she could with dinner party chatter by lapsed Catholics about the symbolism of the consecrated Host, finally exploded, "Well, if it's a symbol, to hell with it." Recounting the incident to a friend years later, she added: "That was all the defense I was capable of but I realize now that this is all I will ever be able to say about it, outside of a story, except that it is the center of existence for me; all the rest of life is expendable."

O'Connor saw herself as a writer who wrote to serve God. "You do not write the best you can for the sake of art," she told an aspiring writer, "but for the sake of returning your talent increased to the invisible God to use or not use as he sees fit." As her own work makes clear, this doesn't mean being pietistic or avoiding subjects that are controversial or even shocking. A committed Catholic writer need fret about that only up to a certain point. "When the book leaves your hands, it belongs to God. He may use it to save a few souls or to try a few others, but I think that for the writer to worry about this is to take over God's business."

And the cross? For much of her not very long life, Flannery O'Connor was seriously, painfully ill. As far as we can tell, her faith grew as a result of the experience. "What people don't realize is how much religion costs," she wrote five years before her death. "They think faith is a big electric blanket, when of course it is the cross."

But the clearest statement of her beliefs on this score doesn't concern her own case — at least, not directly — but that of a little girl named Mary Ann.

One day in the spring of 1960 O'Connor got a letter from the sister superior of Our Lady of Perpetual Help Free Cancer Home, an Atlanta institution operated by a community of Dominican nuns called the Servants for Relief of Incurable Cancer. Their foundress was Rose Hawthorne Lathrop, daughter of the novelist and story writer Nathaniel Hawthorne.

The letter contained an unusual request: Would O'Connor write the story of a child, Mary Ann, who'd come to stay with the sisters when she was three and remained until her death at age twelve? Though hideously disfigured by cancer, she possessed a beauty of soul that deeply impressed everyone who knew her. "After one meeting one never was conscious of her physical defect but recognized only the beautiful brave spirit," the sister superior wrote.

O'Connor declined. But she did look into Mary Ann's story, was deeply impressed, and urged the sisters to write the story themselves. The result was a little book called *A Memoir of Mary Ann,* published in 1961 with O'Connor's help and with an introduction by her.

This introduction is a remarkable piece of writing. On a visit to the sisters, she recalled, one of them asked her why she wrote about the grotesque. As she struggled for an answer, another visitor spoke up. "It's your vocation too," he told the sister. O'Connor commented:

This opened up for me also a new perspective on the grotesque. Most of us have learned to be dispassionate about evil, to look it in the face and find, as often as not, our own grinning reflections with which we do not argue, but good is another matter. Few have stared at that long enough to accept the fact that its face too is grotesque, that in us the good is something under construction. The modes of evil usually receive worthy expression. The modes of good have to be satisfied with a cliché or a smoothing down that will soften their real look. When we look into the face of good, we are liable to see a face like Mary Ann's, full of promise.

But promising what?

She and the Sisters who had taught her had fashioned from her unfinished face the material of her death. The creative action of the Christian's life is to prepare his death in Christ. It is a continuous action in which this world's goods are utilized to the fullest. . . . Mary Ann's diminishment was extreme, but she was equipped by natural intelligence and by a suitable education, not simply to endure it, but to build upon it. She was an extraordinarily rich little girl.

Mary Ann was rich in her vocation, as Flannery O'Connor was in hers. As in fact, we can say without exaggeration, each of us and all of us are in ours.

ABOUT THE AUTHORS

Germain Grisez is the *Flynn* Professor of Christian Ethics at Mount Saint Mary's College, Emmitsburg, Maryland, a chair he has held since 1978. Grisez was born in University Heights, Ohio, in 1929, and married Jeannette Selby in 1951. The couple had four children and are the grandparents of thirteen and great-grandparents of five. Grisez's doctorate in philosophy is from the University of Chicago (1959). Working with Joseph Boyle and John Finnis, he has developed and extensively applied the theory of natural law sketched out by St. Thomas Aquinas. Besides books on contraception, abortion, euthanasia, and nuclear deterrence, as well as other books and many scholarly articles, Grisez has published three volumes of an up-to-date, systematic treatment of Catholic moral theology, *The Way of the Lord Jesus:* volume one, *Christian Moral Principles* (1983); volume two, *Living a Christian Life* (1993); and volume three, *Difficult Moral Questions* (1997). He is currently working on the fourth and final volume of the series: *Clerical and Consecrated Service and Life.*

Russell Shaw is a writer living in Washington, D.C. He was born in Washington in 1935 and received a Master's degree in English literature from Georgetown University in 1960. In 1958, he married Carmen Carbon; they have five children and eight grandchildren. From 1956 to 1966, Shaw worked as a journalist. From 1966 to 1969, he was director of information and publications of the National Catholic Educational Association, from 1969 to 1987, press secretary of the Catholic bishops' conference of the United States, and from 1987 to 1997, director of information of the Knights of Columbus. He is author or co-author of sixteen books, including three written in collaboration with Germain

Grisez: *Beyond the New Morality: The Responsibilities of Freedom, Fulfillment in Christ: A Summary of Christian Moral Principles*, and the present volume. Shaw is Washington correspondent of *Our Sunday Visitor*, editor of *The Pope Speaks*, and a consultor of the Pontifical Council for Social Communications.

INDEX

Notes

Notes

Notes

Notes

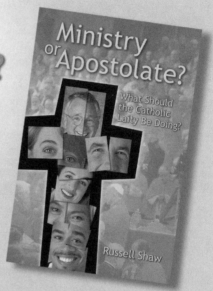

Our Sunday Visitor ...
Your Source for Discovering
the Riches of the Catholic Faith

Our Sunday Visitor has an extensive line of materials for young children, teens, and adults. Our books, Bibles, pamphlets, CD-ROMs, audios, and videos are available in bookstores worldwide.

To receive a FREE full-line catalog or for more information, call **Our Sunday Visitor** at **1-800-348-2440, ext. 3**. Or write **Our Sunday Visitor** / 200 Noll Plaza / Huntington, IN 46750.

Please send me ___ A catalog
Please send me materials on:
___ Apologetics and catechetics
___ Prayer books
___ The family
___ Reference works
___ Heritage and the saints
___ The parish

Name _____
Address _____ Apt._____
City _____ State _____ Zip_____
Telephone (   ) _____

A39BBABP

Please send a friend ___ A catalog
Please send a friend materials on:
___ Apologetics and catechetics
___ Prayer books
___ The family
___ Reference works
___ Heritage and the saints
___ The parish

Name _____
Address _____ Apt._____
City _____ State _____ Zip_____
Telephone (   ) _____

A39BBABP

OurSundayVisitor

200 Noll Plaza, Huntington, IN 46750
Toll free: **1-800-348-2440**
Website: www.osv.com